FOURFOLD

KINGDOM

OF

GOD

Gerald Paul Kooyers

ISBN-13: 979-8698315834

ISBN-10: 8698315834

Published by: MORIA CORPORATION
                  Riggins, Idaho
                  UNITED STATES OF AMERICA

DEDICATION

This BOOK is dedicated to all those of mankind who would endeavor, to seek, to study, to know, and to understand THE KINGDOM OF GOD that exists in that most inner essence of humankind, called in modern translations of the Bible, heart.

And to my wife of three score plus years, Geneva Helene Westra. My Lord Jesus provided me with a most marvelous wife. The scriptures say lands and houses come from parents, but a good wife is from the Lord. Very, very true. Geneva has been a most wonderful wife, and my life most likely would have been a complete mess without her continuing stabilizing presence all the years of our marriage. She, like her own mother, has a marvelous capacity to love, especially to love her children, grandchildren, and great grandchildren, and yes, even me, her husband. And, of course, she loves the Lord Jesus. She also had the good fortune to have been brought up in a Christian home, educated in Christian schools, and learned the great, very powerful, Biblical truths of the Reformed Faith from her parents, church, and school.

And to all those of mankind who would endeavor, to seek, to study, to know, and to understand the rule of God in the Universe.

Gerald Paul Kooyers
January 2021

ACKNOWLEDGEMENTS

My grateful appreciation is disposed upon my dear Lord-Jesus-loving sister, now with the Lord Jesus, Marcia Jane Kooyers Davis, who had the insight, and so gave me the inspiration to understand, that the Tabernacle of the Israelites in the Wilderness was a pre-incarnate representation of Jesus Christ.

CREDITS

Many thanks for proof reading and editorial comments go to Audry Adkins, wife of Russ Adkins, Pastor of the Gem Community Church, in Emmitt, Idaho.

Many thanks go to my nephew Dave Kooyers, Pastor of the Valley Bible Fellowship, an Independent Bible Church in Boonville, California, for his proof reading and editorial comments of a biblical and theological nature.

I thank Professor Richard Muller, professor of physics at the University of California at Berkeley, for writing such an inspiring book, *The Physics of Time*. A time way back when I was a physics graduate student, I studied quantum mechanics with the teaching of Luis Alvarez. Luis, subsequently, became Muller's thesis advisor. Alvarez, a spectacular experimentalist not only in physics, but archeology as well, is the only professor I ever remember from college days.

The rule of Jesus Christ is supreme. "He (Jesus Christ) is the image of the invisible God, the firstborn of all creation. For by Him all things were created, both in the heavens and on the earth, visible and invisible, whether thrones or dominions or rulers or authorities---all things have been created through Him and for Him. He is before all things and in Him all things hold together." (Colossians 1:15-17)

PREFACE

This book is a one volume of a revised new edition of three books written and published by the same author combined into one volume. The first is, *"Christ Rules in Four Realms"*, published in August 2014. The second is *"Hearts of Understanding and the Demise of American Culture"*, published in August in 2015. The third is, *"Jesus' Mysterious Space-Time Universe"*, published in August 2017.

The first book, *"Christ Rules in Four Realms"*, presents the Tabernacle of the Hebrews as a pre-incarnate representation of Jesus Christ. The tabernacle portrays, through four areas of space occupation, Jesus Christ as a four realm, fourfold absolute ruler in the all-encompassing four --- Heart, Spirit, Soul, and Body. Since Jesus Christ is a man, yet a godman, then all of mankind are also individuals with a fourfold nature of heart, spirt, soul, and body.

The second book, *"Hearts of Understanding and the Demise of American Culture"*, offers proof of these fourfold understandings.

The third book, *"Jesus' Mysterious Space-Time Universe"*, explains a little of the physics of how Jesus Christ rules and maintains His Kingdom.

The author was educated as a theoretical physicist. He was taught to think for himself and go to first principals as the source for inductive insights into how things work in the universe, rather than to base his research on the doings of other researchers from the past, when looking for new things yet to be discovered. Now, of course, doings of past researches are very useful, but new inventions of new things and the creation of new ideas and devices come out of inductive blue sky imagination.

Similarly, the ideas and development of the concepts in the above books were not obtained from past students of the bible. These ideas are original with the author and he believes they came directly from revelation through Jesus Christ, who is God in the flesh of a man, through the Holy Spirit of God yet inspired by reading the Bible.

The author has made several original scientific discoveries, built original electronic devices that worked, and holds a technical patent, so he understands how original discoveries are made.

Luis Alvarez, mentioned in the Credits above, in retirement joined his son while doing archeological work. Luis observed interesting repeated layers in old deposits of rocks found in several widely scattered regions of the earth. From this came the nemesis theory about the ageing of the earth. This theory indicates that the earth receives huge meteorite showers about every 26 million years when passing through the solar system of the star nemesis.

This would not have been discovered by a geologist. It required a physicist doing archeological work. So too the presentation of the understandings of this book comes from a physicist doing theological work. No theologian in recorded history has ever before figured out the concepts presented in this book.

The author is a lifelong Christian, the son of a highly educated Presbyterian Minister, who very much loved the Bible inspired truth of the Gospel of The Lord Jesus Christ.

Table of Contents

ONE

Four Functional Realms

One of the more intriguing often repeated themes of the Christian Scriptures is the quantity of four. There are four types of trees in the Garden of Eden, a river that becomes four rivers that water the four types of trees, four beasts in the prophesy of Daniel, four creatures with four faces in Ezekiel's vision of God, four horses and four chariots in the vision of Zechariah, and four living creatures that surround the throne of God and the Lamb in the Revelation of the Apostle John. These four creatures call out four horses, four messengers of destiny. So what is this very fundamental theme of four all about?

The Sower Parable

One of the keys to this foursome theme is given to us in Jesus' parable of the sower. (Matthew 13) Jesus tells us in the parable; a sower went out to sow the seed of the Kingdom of God in the hearts of men. Some seed fell alongside the path where the evil one snatched it away. Some fell in rocky places with shallow soil where persecution and affliction caused falling away. Some seed fell among weeds and thorns where the cares of the world and the deceitfulness of riches choked it out. And some seed fell in good soil where it yielded a bountiful crop. Here again, indeed, is a fourfold operation.

Other manifestations of four are the provision of four Gospels in the New Testament, each with a fundamental theme. We live in the four dimensional space time continuum of the created universe. The Book of Revelation tells about the Four Winds of heaven and the Four Corners of the earth.

What could these encompassing foursomes themes all mean? At a very young age, maybe four years or so, I asked my mother, "Where did I come from?" Yes, that is the most profound question of life. Who and what are we and where did we come from? My mother answered, "God gave you to me" --- a very good answer.

The Bible through the Apostle Paul says, "Now may the God of peace Himself sanctify you entirely; and may your spirit and soul and body be preserved complete, without blame at the coming of our Lord Jesus Christ." (I Thessalonians 5:23) Yes, this verse says three life manifestations are to be preserved eternally. Is there a fourth besides the spirit, soul, and body? The good soil, which of a good heart, yields a bountiful crop in the Kingdom of God. Yes indeed, there are four functional manifestations of life, that of body, soul, spirit, and heart.

Realms of Life

The word realm best describes these manifestations. Realms are regions, kingdoms, spheres, domains, within which anything occurs, prevails, or dominates. Thus there are four realms of life. The sower parable gives us the clue to understanding. The evil one dwells and operates primarily in the realm of the spirit. Persecution and affliction operate in the realm of the flesh in the real physical world of the body. Cares of the world and the deceitfulness of riches operate in the mind, the realm of the soul. The good heart is the soil for the seed of the Kingdom.

These four operating functional realms of life suggest a relationship similar to the eigenfunctions of a physical system from mathematical physics. An operating physical system is based on the magnitudes and vectorization of its eigenfunction combinations and components. Similarly all of the functional nature of human life is the sum of all its components derived from the combinations and conundrums of the components of these four functional realms in some kind of composite integration. These realms are interrelated and encompassed. For example, the evil one, although a spirit, seems to be able to operate in three realms --- by occupying a spirit which drives a soul, which directs a body.

Of course, in the normal English language use of the word realm, Christ rules in all realms. But in order to describe and convey the concept presented here, the word realm is used in the sense of unique functional manifestation, to describe the fundamental essence of mankind and then all of its derivatives and combinations.

Tabernacle of Moses

A powerful insight into the four functioning life realms is the Tabernacle of Moses. Focus on the fact that the Bible presents to us God's relationship to fallen man. A real outstanding message about that relationship is given to us in the example of the Tabernacle. (Exodus chapters 25 to 31 and 36 to 40) The Book of Hebrews (chapters 8 to 10) gives us further interpretation and understanding of the meaning of the Moses Tabernacle. The term tabernacle was used by the apostles Paul and Peter as an expression of living among us, as in tabernacle (dwelt) among us. (2nd Corinthians 5:1-4, 2nd Peter 1:13-14 KJV)

Now then consider a very insightful statement made by Jesus recorded in the Gospel of John. Jesus, when he made a scourge of cords and drove out the money changers and animal sellers from the temple of the Jews (which was patterned after the Tabernacle), was asked by the Jews, "What sign do You show us as your authority for doing these things?" Jesus answered them,

"Destroy this Temple, and in three days I will raise it up."
(John 2:15-22)

The text says He was speaking of His body, meaning the Temple, or Tabernacle, or Tent, of his body. In another context with an encounter with Pharisees about Sabbath law, Jesus told His disciples,

"But I say to you that something greater than the temple is here." (Mathew 12:6)

What was Jesus trying to tell us? Jesus was stating the Tabernacle/Temple is a representative pattern of Him. And the book of Hebrews tells us there is a sanctuary and the true tabernacle in the heavenly eternities, and the earthly Tabernacle/Temple built by Moses, and explained by the book of Hebrews, is a shadow pattern of it.

The unique fundamental belief of Christianity is the deity of the man Jesus, God in the flesh, fully God and fully man.

Consider the words of the very early Christian Church in the Nicene Creed.

"I believe in one God, the Father Almighty, Maker of heaven and earth, and of all things visible and invisible.

And in one Lord Jesus Christ, the only-begotten Son of God, begotten of the Father before all worlds; God of God, Light of Light, very God of very God; begotten, not made, being of one substance with the Father, by whom all things were made."

And He tabernacled (dwelt) among us. (John 1:1-5, John 1:14)

Jesus the Temple of God

Again reflect on the words and context of Jesus saying about Himself, "Destroy this Temple and three days I will raise it up". Jesus is saying, "I am the Temple of God." Destroy me by death and in three days I will arise! Like a lot of Jesus' words here is deep profound instruction and meaning for us.

In ancient times temples were used as the place to worship sundry gods. The important message conveyed here is that Jesus is the objective concentration and methodology for the worship of the only true God! Yes, we Christians worship God through Jesus and only through Jesus. Jesus is the Christians temple for worship of God!

Before his death by crucifixion Jesus faced several judicial type trials before Jews and Romans. The Jewish leaders were determined to make an end of Him so were seeking witnesses, even false witnesses who would agree, to give legal testimony for a trial. In his first trial before Annas, and then before Caiaphas, the High Priest with the Sanhedrin, witnesses were called to testify to Jesus' guilt to be worthy of death. The proceedings were looking for some legal way to condemn Him. Witnesses said,

> **"This man stated, 'I am able to destroy the temple of God, and rebuild it in three days.' " (Matthew 26:61)**

Some stood up to give false testimony but said,

> **"We heard Him say, 'I will destroy this temple made with hands, and in three days I will build another made without hands.' " (Mark 14:58)**

So reliable evidence, by two witnesses, according to Jewish law, was presented against Jesus who agreed according to that law, that Jesus had said He was able to destroy the Temple of God and to rebuild it in three days.

Following this, the High Priest Caiaphas then demanded from Jesus to declare under oath,

> **"I adjure You by the living God, that you tell us whether you are the Christ, the Son of God". (Matthew 26:63-64)**

Jesus' answer was, as you say, yes I am. Then Jesus added,

> **"Hereafter, you will see the Son of Man sitting at the right hand of power, and coming on the clouds of heaven."**

Caiaphas then tore his clothes and declared we do not need any more witnesses.

And so, yes, in the trial before the Sanhedrin, the governing Jewish body under the Roman lordship, Jesus was condemned to death for saying and claiming that He is the Temple of God, confessing that He is the Son of God, the Messiah of God, and stating He has awesome eternal power at the right hand of God! That Jewish system of law under the High Priest accepted Jesus' confession and put Him to death with Roman acquiescence and Roman power.

Wow!   Jesus is the Temple of God!   Truly Jesus is the fulfillment of the picture/pattern of the Tabernacle. Thus Jesus is our own Temple/Tabernacle, and it is to Him we go for worship of God. And then, the Bible teaches that yes, we too, the believing people of God, are somehow woven together in the spirit as living stones into the vast spiritual temple of God, as the Spirit of God lives within each of us Christians who believe in Jesus Christ as their Lord and Savior. As we are all built together as spiritual stones into this spiritual temple of God, Jesus is the cornerstone. (I Corinthians 3:16, 2nd Corinthians 6:16-18, Ephesians 2:21. I Peter 2:4-8)

Pattern of the Temple of God

To give us a little deeper understanding of all this think about the pattern of the Moses Tabernacle. What was the meaning and purpose of it and the subsequent temples? Our understanding will come about by perceiving what the furniture, the tent building and courtyard represent. Let's start from the outside and proceed to the inside. God commanded Moses to be very careful and to make the tabernacle exactly as the pattern he was shown on the mountain where God talked directly with Moses. So God is communicating to us something very important. However, it is very interesting that when God gave the instructions to Moses, God started with the deepest inside part, the Ark, within the tabernacle and worked His way outward.

A man entered the courtyard through a gate on the east side. The entire tabernacle and courtyard was surrounded by a set of tent type walls hung on pillars. The entire tabernacle was portable. The Israelites while they wandered in the desert wilderness for forty years carried it along with them as they moved from place to place. The courtyard was a rectangle. It enclosed an area of about 150 feet by 75 feet. (100 cubits by 50 cubits, the dimensions given in feet are approximate as we now do not accurately know the exact size of a cubit.) Toward the west in the courtyard was a tent building about 15 feet high, 15 feet wide, and 45 feet long (10 cubits by 10 cubits by 30 cubits) made of vertically arranged boards fastened together, overlaid with gold. The roof was of animal skins and woven goat hair mats draped over the walls. (Exodus 26)

The tabernacle tent building itself was ordinary and drab looking on the outside, but very exquisitely beautiful on the inside. When entering the courtyard, the first thing encountered was a large bronze altar for offering burnt sacrifices to God. Halfway between this altar and the tabernacle tent building was a large basin of water for washing the feet and hands of the priests who served God doing the ceremonies.

The tent building had two rooms. A curtain hung between the courtyard and the first room. A more elaborate veil curtain separated the first room from the second inner room. In the first room, called the Holy Place, there was the table for shew bread on the north side. On the south side was a lamp stand. It had three branched lamps extending from each side with a central lamp making it a seven branched lamp made of solid gold. Before the elaborate veil to the inner room was a smaller altar for incense only. The table and incense altar were made of wood overladen with gold. The lamps and the stand were of hammered gold.

The inner room behind the elaborate veil was called the Holy of Holies. It contained two golden angels, called cherubim. They were attached to a top plate that stood above and over a box, called the Ark. The Ark box was overlaid with gold inside and out. The faces of the cherubim looked down toward each other and the Ark. Their wings extended above the Ark and overshadowed it with a small gap between the almost touching wings of the two cherubim. From this gap above and between the cherubim wings, God told Moses, from there God would meet with him and speak to him, and from there after completion of the desert tabernacle God spoke to Moses. (Exodus 25:22, Numbers 7:89)

The Ark was about four feet long, two feet wide, and two feet deep. (2½ by 1½ by 1½ cubits) It had feet and rings with poles inserted for carrying. It was called the Ark of the Covenant and the Ark of Testimony. The lid of gold was of one piece with the gold cherubim. It was called the Mercy Seat and Seat of Propitiation. (Exodus 25:10-22, Exodus 37:1-9)

Inside the Ark were three objects. First was the tablets of stone on which was written the covenant, the law of Ten Commandments by the finger of God, given to Moses on Mount Sinai. There was a golden jar that contained manna, a sample of the white seedy food deposited on the ground for the Israelites to eat while they wandered in the desert wilderness. And there was the Rod of Aaron, a stick of almond tree wood that overnight produced buds, leaves, and almonds so as to prove that Aaron was the chosen High Priest. (Hebrews 9:4) This is a very brief description of the tabernacle.

Jesus is God

When we consider the pattern, the purpose and use, and the contents of the tabernacle, astoundingly, we come to understand a little of whom Jesus is as the Tabernacle/Temple of God. The tabernacle had four enclosed areas: courtyard, Holy Place, Most Holy Place, and the Ark. Those are four interconnected areas enclosed within each other. Areas are places for occupation. These areas suggest a representation of occupation and so suggest four modes, or realms, for a perfect tabernacle, a tent, a place for God to dwell, while among the Hebrews. Jesus by saying He is the Temple/Tabernacle of God is saying that He is the dwelling place for God! **Jesus is saying He is God!** And the representational dwelling place has a pattern of four encompassing places or occupational realms where God through His Son Jesus supremely rules.

Contents of the Rooms and Courtyard

Let us again consider more deeply the contents of the rooms and courtyard in this Mosaic Tabernacle description. Because of the conceptual functional use of the objective furniture, astoundingly, we can come to understand four interconnected life functional realms; define them as four interconnected regions, spheres, domains, modes ---

operations for the complete function of a being. Jesus the perfect man and a dwelling place for God rules perfectly in these four interconnected encompassed functional realms.

For the first realm we perceive and observe the courtyard, which has an altar for burnt sacrifices, and a basin for washing. Here sacrifices and washing occur, which are earthly physical reality functions. We observe bloody sacrifices with our senses, and we observe washing with our senses. These teach us in the physical world. Here is the body, also called the flesh. The courtyard is thus a representation of Jesus in His body. He comes to us as the sacrificial Lamb of God to wash away all our sins. This sacrificial function occurs in the physical world of bodies. The courtyard is, therefore, a pattern representation of Jesus in the flesh, Jesus in a body, Jesus in the physical world.

For the second realm consider within the courtyard the Holy place inside the first curtain, where only the priests could go. Here there was a lamp for light, bread for food, and an altar for burning incense oil resin. The smoke represented prayers. (Revelation 8:3-4, Luke 1:8-10, Psalms 141:2) Here we find a deeper dimension of humanity. Prayer is a function of the mind as part of the soul, the soul being defined as the mind, the will and the emotions. Jesus said, "I am the light of the world." (John 8:12) "I am the bread of life." (John 6:35) – Food and light for the soul. These object representations of food, light, and prayer, are functions that occur in the soul within the body. So in this room, the Holy Place, are functional representations of food for the soul, light for the soul, and prayers of the soul. Jesus prayed many prayers all His life on earth and then in the garden before his crucifixion. So the Holy Place is a pattern representation of the soul functions of the perfect man Jesus with the perfect soul.

In the Holy of Holies, the inner room behind the elaborate veil, were two cherubim with the gap between their wings, (Exodus 25:22) and the Ark. The closed veil and the presence of the cherubim signify this is a spiritual place, the functional room of the spirit, a third realm. This room was entered only once a year on the Day of Atonement by the High Priest alone. If he did not create a cloud of smoke by burning two handfuls of finely ground fragrant incense on a censor full of burning coals from the altar, and bring the smoke and the blood of the bull sacrifice for his sin and the sin of the Israelites, he would die. In the midst of the smoke he sprinkled the blood of the sacrificed bull with his finger seven times in the front and east of the mercy seat which is on the Ark. Then he brought the blood of a goat for the atonement of the nation. (Leviticus 16:1-20) When reading the book of Hebrews (Hebrews 9:3-4) and then comparing it with the Exodus rendering, (Exodus 30:1-10) one perceives the insight that the High Priest brought the incense altar with him or moved the veil past the incense altar when he entered the Holy of Holies within the veil. This is illustrative of the understanding that prayers generated in the mind as part of the soul, have a spiritual dimensional quality and flood the spirit. Inside this Most Holy spirit room is the Ark.

A fourth realm is represented by this Ark. It is like a little room within a room. The contents of the Ark tell us what is the functional representation of the Ark. On the tablets of stone are written the governing principals of life. These principals are reduced to an irreducible minimum and are called the law, also called the covenant. The jar of manna indicates food, so God is providing spiritual inner sustenance. The Rod of Aaron proved Aaron was chosen as High Priest.

Thus the Ark, within the spirit room, tells us of the most perfect inner essence of the being of the man Jesus. In the modern translations of the Bible this is called the heart. The Aaron Rod gave proof of being chosen, so it is a symbol of being chosen by God. All of this Ark content is a representation of the perfect functions of the perfect heart, that most inner essence, that most inner being, of the perfect man Jesus.

The Ark box contents tell us the functions of the heart, the vocation of the heart. These are the true driving principals of life, the perfect commitment to follow God with spiritual input from God in the form of perfect spiritual manna food, and evidence provided by God of being chosen, the Son of God, the perfect man Jesus.

In the above described four realms, Jesus, the perfect man, functioned perfectly. Jesus Christ was crucified on the cross for stating he was the Christ, the Son of God, the Messiah. John the Baptist presented Jesus to the world as the Lamb of God. Jesus as a sacrificial Lamb, died, was buried in a tomb, and rose from the grave on the third day. He entered and passed through the perfect tabernacle in the heavenly eternities. (Hebrews 9:11-14) Jesus alone, among those of mankind, has the perfect fourfold being that functions perfectly, and then rules supremely in four interconnected encompassed realms of life. The Mosaic Tabernacle, a dwelling place for God, portrayed ahead of time the coming of the Lord Jesus Christ as the Messiah, the Savior of the world.

When Jesus died on that cross, the veil separating the Most Holy Place from the Holy Place in the temple in Jerusalem was rent in two from top to bottom. (Matthew 27:51) Thus the doorway into the heavenly eternities is disclosed to all believers as Jesus Flesh, Jesus in his Body, Jesus as the Lamb of God, passing into and through the tabernacle of the heavenly eternities.

Jesus is thus our own Tabernacle/Temple of worship. He, Jesus, brought Himself to His sacrificial death on the cross. This, therefore, describes the essential representation of Jesus, the perfect man, functioning perfectly in four interconnected, encompassing realms.

I borrow the eigenfunction concept from mathematical physics, and state that Jesus Christ is the living, "whole system", for the connecting of mankind to God. He, Jesus Christ, is The Eigenfunction of the whole of everything (both created and uncreated) -- body, soul, spirit, and heart.

And then in some additional words to complete this marvelous anomalous picture, let me say again, Jesus connects and supremely rules in the whole of physical creation including all of the multi-universes.

He supremely rules and knows and understands everything in the realm of imaginations and thinking of all souls. He supremely rules in the whole realm of all the vast spiritual forces and persons. He understands and supremely rules over the vast in number inner essences of all beings. In modern translations of the Bible these are called hearts. He intimately knows the heart of every man and woman. Those hearts that are cleansed (I Corinthians 6:11, Titus 3:5, Psalm 51:10, Hebrews 10:22) belong to Him for eternal fellowship.

What an amazing picture. Jesus, a man fully human like us, yet fully God, God in the flesh, has become our Savior High Priest. He knows all our weaknesses and inadequacies. He ascended from the dead, entered and passed through the eternal Holy of Holies in the tabernacle of the heavens, and as a gift to mankind, sprinkled his own eternal life giving blood on each one of our believing human hearts so as to make us believers perfect before God.

TWO

In The Image of God

What is Man?

Yes, that is the most profound question of all time. At a very young age, about four years, I asked my mother, "Where did I come from?" She said, "God gave you to me". That is a very good answer. But I have never been completely satisfied with that answer. We humans, what are we?

We are more than an animal. We have a sense of eternity – that life is more than eating, sleeping, sexual satisfaction, animal herd encounters with fellow humans, and then death.

Mankind over time has searched for answers. Men have built pyramids, made gods of graven images called idols, searched, and made many studies in the course of living, looking to find answers.

Your writer is a Christian, raised as a Christian from when a child, even as a baby, and was taught the Reformed Faith of his forefathers. I hold the Christian Bible in very high esteem. I was educated to be a theoretical physicist. I went to the Bible for answers.

That in itself would not be an adequate reason to expect to find real truthful answers in the Bible. Therefore, I reached back in my experience to determine objective personal truth. What happened as I studied and slowly understood the writings of the Bible, a very profound thing occurred.

The Christian Life

One does not really understand the joy of swimming in the Salmon River here alongside my home until one swims during the hot summer day in the nice wonderfully cool Salmon River of Idaho.

So too is the Christian life. As one immerses oneself in the Christian life, as one reads and understands the Bible, as one believes the Bible, as one believes the truth of Jesus Christ, the Spirit of Jesus Christ becomes a real part of that one's life.

Then there is this interplay of life in this body of flesh, the thinking going on in one's soul, and the observation of a profound external force different from one's body and soul, most powerfully directing the course of one's life. This is a profound mystery. But this does not make the process any less true. Life is very powerfully influenced by the interplay of the words of the Bible, understanding the aforementioned interplay, and the result; so that God's working in one's life becomes not so much as to be obvious, but nevertheless, here and real.

Hereby you have my testimony. God is real and the interplay in the author's life of God moving and directing is real. This omnipotent God is the Lord Jesus Christ.

In this book I present my answers as to what is life and how life ought to be lived. The Bible is a very profound book. It was written by men inspired by the Holy Spirit of God. Men have translated it in various ways. Truth is often obscured. One must interpret and really work hard to understand the Bible. The Bible is its own interpreter. Interpreting and understanding is not easy, and many false teachers have twisted sundry writings and teachings to support their efforts to exploit their fellow humans for lucre.

Not to Make Money

I have no desire for my books to make money. On occasion I have made a ton of money, so I have been there. I write it for posterity. I write it for those few who seek truth. I write it because I believe the Spirit of God has directed me to do so. I write it to leave the ideas in your hands, dear reader, and leave the ideas in your mind, so you can come to intimately know and love your creator God, the Lord Jesus Christ.

God commanded Moses as he led the people of Israel out of Egypt, when they camped in the wilderness, to build the tabernacle, a tent like structure described in the first chapter. God said he would dwell there among the Israelites and talk to Moses their leader, from the gap between the wings of two cherubim. Two hammered gold images of cherubim, spiritual beings, were attached to a plate of gold which served as a lid to a box. The lid was called the Mercy Seat and the box was called the Ark of the Covenant. The wood box was overlaid with gold inside and outside; the gold lid had the cherubim attached. Moses was to put this into a tent called the tabernacle. All was to be demounted and carried with them when they wandered in the wilderness.

Similarly, you too, can carry the Spirit of God with you, within your spirit, as you wander through the wilderness of life.

This first chapter established that the Mosaic tabernacle was a shadow picture representation of the pre-incarnate Jesus Christ. In Christian understanding, Jesus Christ is God in the flesh of a man. Jesus is both fully God and fully man. Christian theology derived from the Bible states that God is one God in three persons, God the Father, God the Son Jesus Christ, and God the Holy Spirit.

The Christian Scriptures say that man was created in the image of God. Being made in God's image means not only is man a moral being, having the quality of a moral nature in a similar sense as God, but the pre-incarnate Jesus Christ shadow pictured by the tabernacle, is a shadow picture representation of the composite individual man as well. This is perhaps so obvious it needs not to be said, as Jesus, of course, was fully a man who walked around on the earth like any man. So we all are man just as Jesus is of man, and we have a four-fold being like Jesus.

So each man (each woman, too, as in these writings the generic form of the word man means women as well as men and as the word has been historically used in the English language) has a fourfold being, that of heart, spirit, soul, and body.

What word would best describe these fourfold manifestations? Realms are regions, kingdoms, spheres, domains within which anything occurs, prevails, or dominates. Eigenvector is a word from mathematical physics. Quantum physics is described in terms of eigenvalues and eigenvectors. Quantum physics is basic to all chemistry and consequently, basic to all drugs and chemicals for modern living. Similar to the operation of the eigenvector concept is the fourfold nature of mankind. Therefore, let there be four realms of life.

A physical operating system is based on the magnitudes and vectorization of its eigenfunction combinations and components. Similarly all of the functional operation of human life is the sum of all its components derived from the combinations and conundrums of the components of these four functional realms in some kind of composite integration. These realms are interrelated and encompassed. For example, the evil one, although a spirit, seems to be able to operate in three realms - by occupying a spirit which drives a soul which directs a body. The evil one, as understood from reading the Hebrew/Christian Scriptures, is apparently a spiritual being, a fallen angel that God created and yet permits to operate in the spiritual realm

An excellent example showing the fourfold realm relationship is the sower parable of Jesus. Jesus said in His parable a sower goes out to sow seed of the Kingdom of God in the hearts of man. Some seed fall on the path where birds come and eat them. Some seed fall onto rocky places with no depth of soil and so have no growth. Some seed fall into soil where weeds and thorns choke them out. Some seed fall in good soil where they grow and produce much fruit.

Jesus interpreted his own fourfold parable. Carrion birds are a symbol of evil so the evil one gets the seed on the path. The seed that fell in the rocky places with no depth subsumed to affliction and persecution such as occur in the real life of the body of flesh. Cares of the world and the deceitfulness of riches are thoughts which happen in the mind, as represented by the weeds and thorns where fruit production is choked out. The seed that produced thirty, sixty, and one hundred fold fall into good soil, that of a good heart.

The evil one dwells and operates primarily in the realm of the spirit. Persecution and affliction operate in the realm of the flesh in the real physical world of the body. Cares of the world and the deceitfulness of riches operate in the mind, the realm of the soul. The good heart is the soil for the seed of the Kingdom which produces much fruit. These four operating functional realms of life suggest a relationship similar to the eigenfunctions of a physical system from mathematical physics. So hereinafter the term realm is used to refer to that four-fold foundational functional existence of all of the life of man.

Fourfold realms are a theme given again and again in the Bible. First in the Garden of Eden, then in the Tabernacle of Moses, the visions of Ezekiel, the visions of Daniel, the presentation of the four Gospel books of the Bible, the Book of Revelation of John, and the development of the Christian Church in its first 70 years.

The Biblical evidence of the pattern of four realms is overwhelming. The goal of this writing is to describe some of this evidence and to convince you of life in four realms, and so to give you understanding of the nature and structure of man, who, of course, was created in the image of God.

So, if this four realm stuff is all true, what effect does it have on the life of man? That is indeed a mystery I have struggled with for a long time. Of what use is it? The author has been asked that several times. The author confesses he does not know. Like a mountain climber said when he was asked why he climbed mountains, "I climb mountains because they are there to climb." I have climbed a few mountains myself, so I understand that allegory. On a nice day the view from the top is fantastic.

In my lifetime I have contributed some significant scientific findings to the world of electronic engineering. I have also created a commodity trading scheme based on computer technology, advanced for its time making clients a lot of money. All these accomplishments resulted in things to be seen in the real world, that of observation, testing, and proof. Four realm theory is stuff out into the intellectual ether realm where the results of theory cannot be tested in the real world before they are put into practice. Yet four realm theory is the most significant contribution to humankind from all of my life, in that it resulted from revelation from God, through only the Holy Scriptures. This came about as a result of asking God, the Lord Jesus Christ, a man like all of us of the human race, yet very God of very God, for the revelation and thus the understanding.

An apology is given for not seeking and so conceiving the four realm theory when young and in the prime of life. Then powers of reasoning and memory were ten times better. Solid logical proof of many of the assertions and conclusions herein are not properly developed since productivity and mental strength have attenuated with age. Nevertheless, the assertions and conclusions are very true. You will be blessed if you work hard to understand them.

Yes, I believe I was given this imperative to document. This is my calling for the cause of my Lord Jesus Christ, who in all of my life has lead me, comforted me, protected me, delivered me from my stupid idiotic sins, and redeemed me for life eternal. How can I not obey this imperative?

This writing came about because I read the Bible once in a while. I also spent my most formative years studying physics and engineering. I slaved away for a time at a most marvelous educational institution created by man in the Golden Age of the United States of America, the University of California. I worked almost every hour I was awake and not sleeping at studying. I was like a consumed slave pushing rocks up the slope of a pyramid being built for a Pharaoh king day after day. It was back breaking, laborious, mind numbing, and very fatiguing work. Very fortunately, I had roots in Puritan type Reformed Christianity, so I worked only six days a week and went to church and played and socialized on the seventh day. Thus I repeatedly, marvelously, recuperated from such abject painful slavery. But in so doing, I received a most marvelous education so when I read the Bible, the Lord shows me inductive patterns that seem to have unusual meaning that I had never read about before in books and magazines of a Christian nature.

I confess that my first inkling at a foursome thing was given to me by my brother, Orneal, who is nine years older than me and has been a mentor when I was young. Neal, as he prefers to be called, was called of the Lord to go to Papua New Guinea and translate the Bible into indigenous languages. Neal obeyed and with his family ministered many long years in the hot, humid, terrible, mosquito infested, swamps of Papua New Guinea.

A very fine pastor at the Berkeley Presbyterian Church, Earl Palmer, preached that not only does the Lord Jesus forgive you of your sins, but also forgives you of your bad theology. Yes, the Lord is gracious, and will, I pray, forgive me of any and all of my bad theology.

I have read some of the writings of Watchman Nee[1] who spent twenty years, until it was time for him to die, in a Chicom Chinese prison dungeon because of his Christian faith, yes, a martyr for the Lord. Watchman suggests that there are seasons in a Christian's life where sometimes the Lord uses one for the Kingdom, and sometime seasons where the Lord passes on and does not use that same one. This also is a great mystery.

I spent most of my life trying to make money. Sometimes I succeeded in that. However, through the trials and vicissitudes of life, I am now considered to be financially poor, but I assure you, I am very richly blessed by the Lord Jesus, and the season has arrived for me to write. This work is a work motivated by my Lord Jesus. My prayer is that it may be productively used by the Kingdom of Jesus Christ. May it assist to bring many, many people of this race of mankind into that Kingdom.

This perhaps is a very unusual book. The Bible begins with an account of trees and rivers in the Garden of Eden and the creation of man. This book deals with this, continues on with several visions of God, and develops the four realm fourfold understanding of mankind. Extensive Bible proof is given of the realm concept and its application to the life of man.

The book then goes on to deal with moral corruption and its ramifications. Descriptions of early American cultures provide an insight into their demise in terms of moral corruption. The rule of God is considered and looked at and reflected on in terms of non-linear systems. An example of the modern depth of false teaching in the Christian Church is presented and then the consequences of the wrath of God on such false teaching. The marriage relationship is examined and the Biblical concept of the merging of two into one is a little analyzed. The extent of moral corruption of the marriage relationship in America driving the descent of the present culture into destruction is then condemned as a very wicked evil. Subsequent chapters deal with the nature of the created universe, space-time and quantum physics. Quantum physics establishes free will and the mystery of entanglement and eternity are presented. Last a presentation of the whole Christian vision of life for the mature real believer Christian is mandated.

This is a serious book, which if you study it carefully; you may gain insight into what is happening to the modern human race and the country of the United States of America as you live out your life. If you are not a Christian perhaps you will give serious consideration to the claims of Jesus Christ.

THREE

Beginnings

Genesis and the Garden of Eden

From the Bible, the Book of Genesis (2:4-7) we read:

> "This is the account of the heavens and the earth when they were created, in the day that God made earth and heaven. Now no shrub of the field was yet in the earth, and no plant of the field yet sprouted, for the Lord God had not sent rain upon the earth, and there was no man to cultivate the ground. But a mist used to rise from the earth and water the whole surface of the ground. Then the Lord formed man of dust from the ground, and breathed into his nostrils the breath of life, and man became a living being."

So, that is the beginning of man. A little dust from the earth and spirit from the breath of God, which merge, and a living being, a living soul in some translations, results in man! Now this, of course, is a very terse summery of that operation and God spares us all the details.

We are probably very fortunate that God spares us the details. The Bible was written to be time invariant. That is, the Bible needs to be understood by all cultures over all time periods. The creation event and the beginning of man needed to be described in terms that each culture could understand. Ancient Israelites would not have understood modern scientific theories. So we too, like them, if God had provided all the details as to how God in scientific terms made man and God's universe, we moderns would not understand. It is bad enough that we get inkling when thinking about quantum mechanics, as quantum mechanics is almost impossible to understand even now in these present times. Imagine if God had provided all the details. Would you or even our best scientists understand it?

Probably one of the most difficult things to understand is the DNA molecular coding system of plants and animals. How was this system thought up and implemented?   How do all the microscopic engines in each cell operate and how were they designed?   Indeed the whole system will probably not be understood by mankind for a long time and then only if the return of the Lord Jesus is long delayed.

Some will suggest that God created it and it just happened without any process - that everything just came into being. This puts the whole operation of creation into the realm of imagination. In other words, imagining something makes it happen and makes reality. This makes it, it meaning the universe, a spirit happening and not something that is happening in the real physical world of processes. That, I believe, robs God of His glory! It is a very glorious thing to make a universe and create man to live within it. If all of man life is just imagining it, then there is no real physical process of a thing occurring in time and space, and then time and space are all imaginary.

Happenings with no processes are very contrary to the whole theme of the Bible. Many, many passages of the Bible describe God fashioning something like a skilled craftsman would. God made it like a skilled pottery maker. God formed the earth out of water and by water according to the Apostle Peter. There are many such passages.

The most terrible resulting consequence of such an imaginary universe would be that spiritual forces, such as Satan and his evil demons, would have direct access to each man person within it. Man living in time and space, a physical place separate from the spirit realm, provides a tremendous protection over each man person as spiritual forces can only directly operate in the spirit realm.

This means, as will be demonstrated in this writing, that physical forces operate only in the physical realm and spiritual forces operate only in the spirit realm. The soul realm interconnects the two so that as the soul receives spirit input, the soul handles and processes it and then the soul may or may not decide to make things happen in the physical realm as a result of spirit input. The soul thus becomes a separate thing from physical reality and a separate thing from the spirit realm. The soul realm interconnects the two.

So to continue in the Bible account, after making man, God planted a garden for man to keep and cultivate. We read (Genesis 2:8-9):

> "The Lord God planted a garden toward the east, in Eden, and there He placed the man he had formed. Out of the ground the Lord God caused to grow every tree that is pleasing to the sight and good for food, the tree of life also in the midst of the garden, and the tree of knowledge of good and evil."

So God planted a garden in the East in a place called Eden, as a place for man to live and cultivate. Subsequent scriptures tell us about four rivers that were to water this Garden of Eden where four kinds of trees were to grow. It is possible this story describing Eden is an allegory. But much scripture is an account of real events and has been recorded for us to receive an allegorical meaning. This is meant to instruct us and to develop in us understanding about God so we become beings who come to know and love God.

The four kinds of trees placed in Eden are, first, providing food for physical life, second, pleasing to the eye; third, tree of knowledge; and fourth, tree of life. The rivers came from one source, seem to have divided into four rivers, and then water, which gives life, to the Garden of Eden.

An important question is: Why does God expend words about trees and rivers in the beginning of the Bible, describing the beginning of creation and the beginning of mankind? One might think there is far more important information to impart to man than stories about trees and rivers. One must conclude these rivers and trees are very important to the understanding of man and man's perception of God from the very beginning.

The meaning of the trees are perhaps more obvious than the rivers. The trees providing food feed man in the physical life, where within this book, I call the first realm of life, life of man in the flesh, life in all of physical creation, life in all the universe existence.

The tree pleasing to look upon appeals to the eye --- eye meaning the spirit. Eye and eyes in the Bible are used as a symbol of spirit. So the tree good to look upon feeds the sense of beauty in man. This tree feeds the spirit; this is the third realm of man for life, life of spirit.

The tree of knowledge feeds life in the second realm, life in the soul, life in all the imaginations, plans, programs, and all things man thinks, creates, and understands.

Then there is the tree of life.

When God formed man he took dust from the earth, from the realm of physical reality, inserted spirit from the realm of spirit into this dust, producing a soul in the second realm, that of thinking, imagining, and of civilization. Now, as will be shown in this account, the spirit realm has deep within it the realm of a thing called the heart, the inner essence of the real ultimate basis of human life in man. That, from the perspective of the presentation of this four realm fourfold understanding, is life in the fourth realm, the life in the inner essence, ultimate inner life with Jesus, giving eternal life.

God understood a great danger here. If the man whom He created could dream up, design, make, or construct almost anything, and man collectively with his fellows is able to do just about anything, then God must include death, the termination of this creature. For if the creature was to live forever and to embark on an evil path, and there were nothing the creature could not accomplish, the result would be disastrous and contrary to God. Therefore, the fruit of the tree of knowledge must have within it the virus or agency of death so that man, as he feeds this soul and develops this latent huge potential in mind and will, and has the capacity to do both good and evil, eventually must be put to death.

To thoroughly establish in your understanding mind this four realm fourfold theory as presented in this book, let's go back, and again consider the beginning of man. The scriptures say the Lord God planted a garden in the East. There He put the man whom He had formed. We have discussed the trees God planted, so now consider the rivers that watered the trees of the Garden of Eden.

Names of places are often used again and again for new places in new locations. In ancient times the names of the rivers of Eden were used again and again by subsequent peoples, the names given to other rivers in other places, and then to places in the land of Mesopotamia. Let's look at the roots of the words used as the names given to the rivers of the Garden of Eden to understand what message God is giving to us about the beginnings of mankind and the Garden of Eden.

The account says a river flowed from Eden and divided into four rivers to water the garden. The root of the word Eden is delight, plain, steppe, or flat area. So the message is, a river flowed from a delightful plain into the garden where the man was placed and there it divided into four rivers to water the garden.

The first of the rivers in the garden was named Pison, or Pishon. The root meaning of that word is to increase, multiply, overflow, or to make grow around the land. The biblical account says the Pishon winds around the whole land of Havilah where there is gold and precious stones. The root meaning of Havilah is circle, land, distant, perhaps sandy. So the river Pishon winds around the very rich land, as indicated by gold and precious stones, of the garden and waters it.

The second river is the Gion, or Gihon. The root meaning of the word Gihon is to burst forth, arise from the east, swift, or impetuous. The Gihon winds through the land of Cush. The root of the word Cush seems to have been indistinct or undefined. Perhaps the meaning is intended to be indistinct so Cush may mean an indistinct place not defined.

The third river is given the name of Hiddekel. The root meaning of this word is active, rapid, vehement, sharp, rapid velocity flow, swift, or arrows, going east. It is on the east side of Asshur, the root meaning of Asshur being a region of vegetation associated with water.

The fourth river is called the Euphrates. The root meaning of this word is sweet river, long river, fruitful river, good to cross over or swim in, or good and abounding river. It is the mightiest of the four rivers.

What are we to make of these four rivers that water the Garden of Eden? Why does God spend time telling us about rivers that water a garden? There is a much deeper meaning to the rivers' names then just geographical locations. The geographic descriptions, if applied to presently existing rivers make no sense at all, since the names have been reused and applied to new rivers subsequently discovered. The character of the land has changed greatly through the centuries as well, and we now have no idea where the Garden of Eden was located.

Realm understanding suggests these four rivers were to water symbolically the four kinds of trees in the garden to provide sustenance to man in Eden. The Pishon, the first river, is symbolic of *watering the trees whose fruit provided food*, sustenance for the physical body, that of the first realm.

The Gihon is symbolic of *watering the trees beautiful to look upon*, trees associated with the spirit of man as it bursts forth, arising from the east, meaning arising from God Himself, swift and impetuous. The Gihon winds around the whole of the land as the spirit of man has no boundary, an indistinct place as the root of the word Cush implies, and is transcendent. So the watering of the spirit of man knows no boundaries. This river is symbolic of watering the trees of the garden that appeal to the third realm, the spirit of man.

The Hiddekel (sometimes translated Tigress), the third river, is symbolic of *watering the trees associated with the soul of man*. This river is active, rapid, vehement, flowing swiftly, like an arrow. East of Asshur name associated with it suggests it has no vegetation of the kind found along a river. It flows to the east, meaning that in being watered and nurtured, the soul of man is to seek God, flowing to the east, or flowing to God. The prefix part of the word means "very." The meaning of the name is very sharp or very rapid. This river is symbolic of watering that tree in the garden – the tree of knowledge. However, with knowledge comes knowing good and evil, and once man knows evil, there is death, the consequence of eating the fruit of this tree of knowledge of good and evil.

The fourth river, called the Euphrates, is symbolic of *watering the tree of life*. The tree of life is watered by sweet water, long life abounding water of the river of life. It is intended to be the mightiest of the four rivers and waters the tree that feeds the fourth realm of man, that of his heart or inner essence, so he will be abounding in love – love of God and love of his fellow creatures.

Of course, the tree of life is symbolic of the Lord Jesus Himself. We, who are fallen creatures, are to absorb the life of Jesus, and to become like him in our life in all the four functional realms.

Thus, from the beginning of scripture, we have a message that man is a functioning foursome or functions in four realms, to be fed by fruit of four kinds of trees, which are watered by four different in application rivers. The conclusion is obvious. Man functions as a foursome fourfold entity. Man has four life manifestations - from which all of life can be composed, even into eternity, the life beyond the life we now live in our physical bodies on the earth. This sets forth our complete functional existence

The astounding thing about this account is the vast encompassing of all of life. Man starts with a four realm being. Man's body is to be nurtured by fruit from trees good for food. The spirit of man is to delight in beauty from trees beautiful to look upon. Then this soul which resulted from the insertion of spirit into dust has placed before it the tree of knowledge of good and evil. But then God said, "Do not eat of it, for if you do, you will surely die."

What a dilemma. Man has this capacity for knowledge with astounding potential, but with knowledge comes death because man then knows evil, is capable of doing evil. And when man does evil he must be put to death.

Then, of course, there is the tree of life. The fruit of that tree brings eternal life. By eating of the fruit of the tree of knowledge of good and evil against the specific command of God, and so then to then receive the sentence of physical death, God then further intervenes, and man is then denied access to the tree of life in the center of the garden. Man is removed from the garden, and cherubim, powerful spiritual creatures, with a flaming sword are placed to guard the way to the tree of life.

So we have man. So we have you and me. Where are we going?

The Vision of Ezekiel

After getting kicked out of the Garden man is sent to wander around in the wilderness of life. Let us pick up the account of this race of man after a considerable time has passed, sometime after a severe trial has occurred in the lives of the Hebrews, a special chosen people of God. The people have been defeated by their enemies and have been exiled to the land of Mesopotamia. The Prophet of God, Ezekiel, is sent to comfort and commiserate with them.

The goal of this writing is to give you an understanding about yourself and a little understanding about God since man is made in the image of God. The Bible has several marvelous descriptions of the Glory of God. Analyzing the Glory of God will give us a little more understanding of man. Consider two descriptions, one of them given to us in the book of Ezekiel and then another one from the book of Revelation of the Apostle John. Again, look at and consider the Glory of God so as to understand something of man.

Here is the quote from the Book of Ezekiel from the New American Standard (NAS) version of the Bible. Some of the translator's supplied words in the original NAS text have been removed. This preserves as much as possible the meaning of the text without having overly much influence of the translators. Of course, all translations are interpretations. The NAS translation used in this book is probably the most accurate translation we have in English. Here follows from the first Chapter of Ezekiel (1:1-2:1):

"Now it came about in the thirtieth year on the fifth day of the fourth month, while I was by the river Chebar among the exiles, the heavens were opened and I saw visions of God. (On the fifth of the month in the fifth year of King Jehoiachin's exile, the word of the Lord came expressly to Ezekiel the priest, son of Buzi, in the land of the Chaldeans, by the river Chebar, and there the hand of the Lord came upon him.)

As I looked, behold a storm wind was coming from the north, a great cloud with fire, flashing forth continually and a bright light around it, and in the midst something like glowing metal in the midst of the fire. Within it there were figures resembling four living beings. And this was their appearance: they had human form; each of them had four faces and four wings. Their legs were straight and their feet were like a calf's hoof, and they gleamed like burnished bronze. Under the wings on their four sides were human hands. As for the faces and wings of the four of them, their wings touched one another, did not turn when they moved, each went straight forward. As for the form of their faces, had the face of a man, all four had the face of a lion on the right and a face of a bull on the left, and all four had the face of an eagle.

Such were their faces. Their wings were spread out above; each had two touching another, and two covering their bodies. And each went straight forward; wherever the spirit was about to go, they would go, without turning as they went. In the midst of the living beings there was something that looked like burning coals of fire, like torches darting back and forth among the living beings. The fire was bright and lightning was flashing from the fire. And the living beings ran to and fro like bolts of lightning.

Now as I looked at the living beings behold there was one wheel on the earth beside the living beings for the four of them. The appearance of the wheels and their workmanship was like sparkling beryl, and all four of them had the same form, their appearance, and workmanship as if one wheel were within another. Whenever they moved, they moved in any of their four directions without turning as they moved. As for their rims they were lofty and awesome, and the rims of all four of them were full of eyes round about. Whenever the living beings moved, the wheels moved with them. And whenever the living beings rose from the earth, the wheels rose. Wherever the spirit was about to go, they would go in that direction. And the wheels rose close beside them; for the spirit of the living beings in the wheels. Whenever those went, these went; and whenever those stood still, these stood still. And whenever those rose from the earth, the wheels rose close besides them; for the spirit of the living beings in the wheels.

Now over the heads of the living beings was something like an expanse, like the awesome gleam of crystal, spread out over their heads. Under the expanse their wings were straight, one toward the other; each one also had two wings covering its body on the one side and one the other. I also heard the sound of their wings like the sound of abundant waters as they went, like the voice of the Almighty, a sound of tumult, like the sound of an army in camp; whenever they stood still, they dropped their wings.

Now above the expanse that was over their heads there was something resembling a throne, like lapis lazuli in appearance; and on which resembled a throne, high up, a figure with the appearance of a man. Then I noticed from the appearance of His loins and upward something like glowing metal that looked like fire all around within it, and from the appearance of his loins and downward I saw something like fire; and a radiance around Him. As the appearance of the rainbow in the clouds on a rainy day, so is the appearance of the surrounding radiance. Such was the appearance of the likeness of the glory of the Lord. And when I saw, I fell on my face and heard a voice speaking. Then He said to me, "Son of man, stand on your feet that I may speak with you!"

What can we understand from this text? Most people's minds fog over and ponder. For years when I read this text, I shook my head and moved on. But really, this text is very, very profound.

Here is a list of things to ponder while you think of the Glory of God:

>Living beings
>Human form
>Four faces – man, lion, bull, eagle
>Four wings
>Human hands on wings
>Moved straight without turning or rotating
>Rims high, awesome, full of eyes
>Spirit in the wheels
>Wheels within wheels
>Appearance of fire, glowing metal surrounding images
>Sound of an army in camp

Consider that glory to be pictured is as something with weight (massiveness), significance, beauty, awesomeness, that is, much wonderful glory. The prophet was to be called to a real, very tough ministry. He would be persecuted, lied about, not believed, rejected, and he would lose his life. He needed to be assured that, no matter what, God would deliver and that God has the capacity to deliver.

So what is the nature of God? Many hands would indicate the ability to do many things, to do much work. Eyes would indicate much seeing and understanding as to know what is going on. Wheels indicate the ability to move great weight anywhere. Wings would indicate ability to go anywhere quickly without the need for a surface to move upon. So God is everywhere, massive, and capable of doing anything, anywhere. Wheels within wheels would indicate that spirit is multi encompassed, things within things, enigmas within enigmas.

Then consider the four beings with four faces; these beings operate to do God's work. These beings function for God by carrying out God's operations. They bolt around like lightning. They can go anywhere and do anything and are everywhere fast and with power and have many eyes and many hands. The face of man indicates activity and power in the affairs in the realm of man. The lion face indicates power to rule. The lion is king of beasts. Christ has been portrayed as the Lion of the Tribe of Judah. The bull face, sometimes portrayed as an ox face, indicates power to do work, to operate in the realm of physical creation where man lives with his body. The eagle face, which does not have a supplied location on the four faced figure, would indicate flying capability, not confined anywhere, so is a figure representation of spirit. These four faces indicate the beings can operate and do things, build things, whatever, in the realms of mankind activities - ruling mankind, mankind work, mankind thinking, and mankind spirits. Yes, these beings operate in the four realms of man's existence.

Ezekiel is given this fuzzy picture of the Glory of God. God is awesome, high and lifted up on a throne, God rules supremely, and God operates through angelic cherubim beings who operate in the realms of the civilization structure of man, the physical body of man in physical creation, the spirit of man, and the inner essence of man, where the man rules his own being. Yes, in the inner essence heart of man, God operates and rules.

God is awesome and sounds like a million man army in camp. God tells Ezekiel, stand on your feet and I will tell you truth about the nature of things, and tell you what you are to do.

There is an interesting description this Prophet Ezekiel has written about cherubim, which are angels of God and serve God directly. Ezekiel describes a scene of the Glory of God where the foursome thing has four faces, that of a man, that of a lion on the right, the bull on the left, and the face of an eagle. But when the cherubim glory is described, they have faces of the cherub, man, lion, and eagle. Therefore, we can conclude that cherubim are also functioning fourfold realm foursomes, the face of the bull being replaced by the face of the cherub when describing cherubim.

So here we have again the four-fold nature of the beings of God's creation where cherubim are functioning foursomes in realms of spirit, soul, and heart, but instead of a body of flesh represented by the bull for mankind, have a body represented by that of a cherub.

Vision of John the Apostle

Consider another word picture of the Glory of God, a shadow presentation of heaven, a word picture painted by the Apostle John, who wrote the Book of Revelation. John describes a throne, high and lifted up, and ONE seated on the throne (Revelation 4 & 5). Around the throne are four living creatures which continuously say, "Holy, Holy, Holy is the Lord God, the Almighty, who was and who is and who is to come," and, "Worthy are you, our Lord and our God to receive glory and honor and power, for you created all things, and because of Your will they existed, and were created."

The Lamb of God appears before the throne, slain since the foundations of the universe were laid. The Lamb has seven horns and seven eyes, which are the seven Spirits of God sent out into all the earth. This is, of course, Jesus Christ, the son of God Himself, the Godman, the Lamb.

Surrounding the Lamb are four living creatures or four living beings covered with eyes all around, indicating they are very powerful spiritual beings and see and understand everything. Surrounding the four living creatures are twenty-four elders, seated on thrones, clothed with white robes, having gold crowns, and holding harps. Surrounding the elders are myriads of angels. In front of the throne is a multitude no man can number, from every tribe, people, nation, and tongue, clothed in robes washed white with the blood of the Lamb, with palm branches in their hands.

What are we to make of this picture? First, it is a picture of the gospel of Christ, the central tenet of the Christian religion. The multitude no man can number are those men and women saved from destruction and judgment, washed clean of their sins by the blood of the Lamb who have been ushered into eternal life to have fellowship with

God through the Lamb, Jesus Christ, a manifestation of God Himself, the third person of our triune God.

Similar pictures of the Glory of God are presented in Old Testament scriptures. It seems we can understand the meaning of thrones and elders and angels, but what are they, and why the four creature beings? These creatures have six wings like angels so they are powerful spiritual beings, but they are around the main throne and the Lamb.

This must also be a message about the four functional fourfold realms through which God's absolute power and omnipotence is projected. John says the first creature appears like a lion, the second like an ox or calf, the third has the face of a man, and the fourth is like a flying eagle. The lion is symbolic of rule or one who rules, representing the functional realm of that inner essence heart of beings which rule, so God's rule is omnipotent in all beings. The ox or calf is a representation of the functional realm of flesh, that of the real world so God projects absolute omnipotent power in the realm of the real physical world of matter, energy, time, and space. The face of the man represents man's civilization – thinking, planning, the doings of mankind, all that takes place in the soul and imaginations of mankind. Here is represented God's rule and projection of absolute power in the functional realm of the thinking souls of beings. The flying eagle represents the spirit realm, acting anywhere, seemingly effortlessly like a soaring eagle. Here also God rules in absolute omnipotent power.

This is the throne of God; the throne represents omnipotent power and control. These four creatures indicate God's supreme absolute power and the modes through which God supremely rules. Yes, God rules supreme in the realm of His physical creation, rules supreme in the minds of man and over all the doings and dreams and thinking of man, rules absolutely in the spirit realm, and then rules absolutely in the hearts of man.

As John watches this scene, the four creature beings picturing God's supreme power in four realms call out four horses. The Lamb opens the seals of destiny. As the first four seals are opened, four horses with riders appear. From the Old Testament scriptures of Zechariah, we understand that horses and riders represent messengers sent out to patrol the earth.

The first creature, that of the lion, says with a voice of thunder, "Come," and the white horse and rider go forth to conquer, the rider with a bow and crown. Later in the book of Revelation, the white horse messenger is identified as an agent of the Kingdom of Jesus Christ. This conquering occurs in the fourth realm, that of the inner essence, or hearts of man. The white horse messenger is adding men and women with its bow and giving them crowns to rule their lives in the Kingdom of Jesus Christ as this messenger patrols the earth.

As the Lamb opens the second seal of destiny, the second creature around the throne with an appearance of an ox or calf, calls, "Come", and a red horse messenger goes out, the rider with a great sword and granted to take peace from the earth --- men killing one another. Men killing one another occurs in the first realm, that of the flesh of the body in the real physical world. The red horse messenger goes forth throughout the earth, giving mankind power to kill as well as to engage in sinful, shameful, acts to destroy one another. Man is given power to corrupt and to become slaves of sin and corruption.

As the Lamb opens the third seal of destiny, the third living creature with the face of a man calls, "Come", and a black horse messenger goes forth, its rider with a scale in his hands, a voice in the center of the living creatures says, "A quart of wheat for a unit of money, and three quarts of barley for a unit of money, and do not damage the oil and the wine."

These are trading transactions. Men trade with one another – men making money and conducting business affairs, men cheating and taking advantage of one another, stealing and defrauding one another. This happens in the second fourfold realm, that of the soul - that of the realm of mind, will, and emotions. Again, this is a source of corruption for mankind.

As the Lamb opens the fourth seal of destiny, the fourth living creature, like a flying eagle, says, "Come", and an ashen horse or pale horse messenger goes forth; the rider named "Death", Hades following with him. Hades is the place of the dead, containing the spirits of the dead. Authority was given to the ashen horse rider to kill with sword, famine, pestilence, and wild beasts. As men and women die of sundry causes, their spirits are collected in Hades.

Ultimate death is death of the spirit, the second death as described later in John's Book of Revelation. In this realm, that of the spirit, ultimate death occurs.

In this vast picture of the Glory of God, the four functional realms, as has been herein suggested, appear. God's Glory demonstrating God's absolute power over everything has four aspects to it, as the four living creatures projecting God's omnipotent power surrounding the throne indicate. Mankind, because they are created in the image of God, also have four functional aspects to their nature; they exists in four realms; they have four modes and/or vectors of life, and then live in four life functional fourfold realms.

Looking at the whole wondrous word picture recorded for us by the Apostle John, the Lamb opens the seals of destiny. The four living creatures serving God call out messengers to go forth into the earth. The messengers in their respective functions of their realms have power to conquer, have power to take peace from the earth, have power to enable men and women to conduct affairs and business, and have power to kill.

Here it seems we have all of the human experience in perspective. Men and women live lives in the flesh, eating, sleeping, consuming, suffering corruption and degradation, and historically, have spent much time killing one another. They trade with one another and some become rich and acquire goods and honor through civilization and competition. They enjoy beauty and become puffed up and proud. They write books, engage in intellectual pursuits, and enjoy the arts.

In all of this vast operation, the spirit of God enters into the spirits of some men and women, washes and purifies their hearts, and they acknowledge and love God. It all seems to be a huge stage play where each human seeks out each one's own destiny. Some choose through faith in Jesus Christ to be washed clean of their sins by the blood of the Lamb and join the multitude before the throne. Others sink into the oblivion of their sins. Some emerge as that multitude before the throne in white robes of righteousness in eternal fellowship with the Lamb; others are left in Hades for the ultimate destruction of their spirits on the day of the final judgment.

That is it! That is the human condition! Yes indeed! Yes! Yes! Yes!

I hope I have convinced you that you are a complex four-fold person, functioning in four realms. The scriptural evidence is overwhelming. Man functions in four realms.

FOUR

Man Lives in Four Realms

Man Created in the Image of God

Man was created in the image of God (Genesis 1:26-27). Let us then take the beautiful representation of our Lord Jesus Christ, portrayed by the tabernacle as described in the first chapter, who after all was fully man and fully God, and now consider mankind.

Mankind became corrupt. Adam and Eve, the first of the created man line chose to deliberately reject the command of God and so eat of the fruit of the tree of the knowledge of good and evil. This fruit had within it the virus or other agency of death as well as now imparting to man the capacity for knowledge and the capacity for doing evil, that is, sin. So, all of mankind is now subject to death.

To alleviate the corruption, men and women, hereinafter called man; in the process of becoming devout Christians have the desire to become like Jesus. It is a profound process. Yes, the goal is to be washed clean of the corruption of sin and then come to intimately know God.

Consider now the four realms of man in the same progression of development God used to instruct Moses on how the Holy Tabernacle in the wilderness, a shadow picture of the pre-incarnate Jesus Christ and, therefore, also a similar shadow picture of man, was to be built. The Lord God in His instructions to Moses, started on the inside (the Ark of the Covenant) and worked to the outside (the courtyard). Consider now the heart, the spirit, the soul, and then the body in that order.

Realm of the Heart

The term "heart" used in English translations of the Hebrew Christian Scriptures, the Bible, refers to the inner essence of one's being, the center of one's being. And, in an anthropomorphic way, God also has a heart. For example, when God was considering the destruction of man by a flood, we read in the book of Genesis (6:5-8):

> "Then the Lord saw that the wickedness of man was great on the earth, and that every intent of the thoughts of his heart was only evil continually. The Lord was sorry that He had made man on the earth, and He was grieved in His heart. The Lord said, "I will blot out man whom I have created from the face of the land, from man to animals to creeping things and to birds of the sky; for I am sorry that I have made them." But Noah found favor in the eyes of the Lord."

The intent of the thoughts of the heart of man is only evil. God's heart was filled with pain and was grieved that he had made man because of all the evil man conceived. After the flood, after the destruction of all mankind except for Noah and his family, Noah built an altar and made an offering to God. Again from Genesis (8:20-21):

> "Then Noah built an altar to the Lord, and took of every clean animal and of every clean bird and offered burnt offerings on the altar. The Lord smelled the soothing aroma; and the Lord said to Himself, "I will never again curse the ground on account of man, for the intent of man's heart is evil from his youth; and I will never again destroy every living thing, as I have done."

The intent of man's heart is evil from his youth. Yet we have the promise here that God will never again destroy mankind so long as the earth exists. So how is God to develop man and deal with the problem of the evil intent of the heart of man?

The Hebrews, that race of man whom God chose to be His special people, if and when they return to Him, were given a promise through Moses in the book of Deuteronomy (30:6):

> "**M**oreover, the Lord your God will circumcise your heart and the heart of your descendants, to love the Lord your God with all your heart and with all your soul, so that you may live."

There we have it. God will circumcise the heart of the repentant Hebrew. Then people may love God with all their heart and soul. The Apostle of Christianity, Paul, a Hebrew, writes in the New Testament book of Romans (2:28-29):

> "For he is not a Jew who is one outwardly, nor is circumcision that which is outward in the flesh. But he is a Jew who is one inwardly; and circumcision is that which is of the heart, by the Spirit, not by the letter; and his praise is not from men, but from God."

Hebrew physical first realm bloody circumcision of the male sexual organ then is an outward act or sign, the cutting of the flesh, corresponding to an inner act by the Spirit of God, to circumcise the heart of the Hebrew.

The Apostle Paul says to mankind in the book of Romans (10:8-10):

> "THE WORD IS NEAR YOU, in your mouth and in your heart"—that is, the word of faith which we are preaching, that if you confess with your mouth Jesus as Lord, and believe in your heart that God raised Him from the dead, you will be saved; for with the heart a person believes, resulting in righteousness, and with the mouth he confesses, resulting in salvation."

So there it is! With our heart, our inner essence being, we believe, and it is counted as righteousness, giving us right standing with God. Our heart, our inner being, then believes that God raised Jesus from the dead.

When a person becomes a Christian, he or she becomes a Spirit washed person, and is given a purified heart, a cleansed heart. They are like the repentant Hebrew with his circumcised heart. The heart, or inner essence, is an essential part of our being from which comes faith, and is the essential driving force deep within our God-loving inner being.

The question is, does each heart of man produce evil intent continuously, or does it produce intent for love of God, resulting in righteousness, and, subsequently, love for fellow human beings?

This is one of the questions to be answered by this writing. Coming to know God is the most singular imperative of all of life. To start to understand something of the God loving heart, consider now the contents of the Mosaic Ark as symbols of what is in the heart of believing man.

The Ark box is a representative picture shadow of the heart, the inner essence being of man. The lid is a plate of pure gold. Gold is a symbol indicating it is of God and indicates the extreme importance and value of the heart. The content inside the Ark, which show a shadow image of what is inside the Christian believer's heart, is first the covenant of the law written on stone, the Ten Commandments, or call them the essence of the ruling principles of life. The Prophet Jeremiah prophesied that in the last days, the days we are now in, and the Christian era, the laws of God would be written on the believer's heart. The New Testament book of Hebrews (8:10-12) quotes Jeremiah:

"This is the covenant that I will make with the house of Israel:

After those days says the Lord:

> I will put my laws into their minds,
> And I will write them on their hearts,
> And I will be their God,
> And they shall be my people,
> And they shall not teach everyone his fellow citizen,
> And everyone his brother, saying, "Know the Lord,"
> For all will know me,
> From the least to the greatest of them,
> For I will be merciful to their iniquities,
> And I will remember their sins no more."

Thus we have the new covenant promised by God. God writes his laws on our hearts.

This is in contrast to the unbelieving heart given in Jeremiah 17:9:

> "The heart is more deceitful than all else and is desperately sick;
> Who can understand it?
> I, the Lord, search the heart, I test the mind,
> Even to give to each man according to his ways,
> According to the results of his deeds."

Again from the New Testament, Matthew 15:19:

> "For out of the heart come evil thoughts, murder, adulteries, fornication, thefts, false witness, slanders."

We have this absolute contrast, this binary dichotomy, either a believing heart, or a deceitful, desperately sick heart.

The second thing inside the Ark is a golden jar containing manna. As we worship God, God feeds our cleansed hearts with spiritual manna. Wandering Israel in the wilderness was provided with manna food, a white coriander seed like substance, appearing on the ground every day, but was not to be gathered on the Sabbath day, the day of rest. Our believing hearts are so also fed daily with spiritual food input from God. When Jesus taught His disciples to pray, He taught them,

"Give us this day our daily bread".

As with a lot of Jesus words, a deep double meaning is provided to man.

There are a lot of double meaning word collections in the Bible. The meaning can be understood as the thrust of the meaning of each word in itself collectively, let's say literally, but then also to have fantastic allegorical meaning. There are collections of words in the Bible that even have a triple meaning, when allegorical pictures are to be presented.

So when we pray what is called the Lord's Prayer, "Give us this day our daily bread," we Christians are not only asking God to provide us food for our physical lives, but we also are praying for spiritual manna food for our hearts.

A remarkable observation about spiritual manna food for the believer is that, just like the manna coriander seed like substance gathered by the Israelites, it must be gathered every day. The Israelites were to go out every day and gather manna. They were to gather as much as each should eat. When they measured it, each had an omer, and he who gathered much had no excess. (An omer is about a tenth of a bushel, maybe five to six pounds) If they tried to save it over to the next day it would spoil and make a stench. We believers, too, are to gather into our hearts spiritual manna food for everyday living.

On the day before the Sabbath rest, however, Israelites were to gather enough for the Sabbath day too, and it did not spoil. What a beautiful picture of our believing Christian life. Every day we are to gather from our life out living in the world, spiritual food for our hearts. On the day of rest God feeds us our spiritual food and we have no need to gather from the world.

The third thing inside the Ark was Aaron's stick of almond wood. There was a disagreement among the Israelites as to why Aaron was chosen as High Priest. Some disputed it, so Moses had the leader of each Israelite tribe make a rod of almond wood. All the rods were then bundled together and placed before the Lord God. In the morning, only Aaron's rod had budded, putting out leaves and almonds, proving that Aaron was chosen as High Priest. This stick in the Ark is a picture of being chosen by God. So in your inner being, your cleansed, purified heart, God has put evidence that you have been chosen by God. You belong to Him. You know you belong to Him, your heart tells you, and yes, yes, you belong to the Almighty Lord God.

Now we have this astounding picture of the shadow image of man, made in the image of God. There the believer's heart, like a valuable box, contains the law of God written upon stone, daily spiritual manna food from God, and evidence from God that He has chosen you to be His.

Understand from this pattern of the Mosaic Tabernacle. Our hearts are a spirit thing but like a box, in the room like thing of our spirit, a little room within a room.

Consider now the room surrounding the heart, the realm of the spirit.

Realm of the Spirit

Jesus gives us some astounding words about how we are to feed upon him, to feed upon His life. He wants us to feed upon Him, the fruit from the Tree of Life, so we will not die, and instead have eternal life. Let's quote Jesus at some length to give an understanding of what Jesus commands the Christian believer to do. Again, the quotes I present are from the *New American Standard* (NAS) version of the Bible, used here by permission.

Jesus said, as recorded in the 6th chapter of the book of John:

> "Truly, truly, I say to you, unless you eat the flesh of the Son of Man and drink His blood, you have no life in yourselves. He who eats My flesh and drinks My blood has eternal life, and I will raise him up on the last day. For My flesh is true food, and My blood is true drink. He who eats My flesh and drinks My blood abides in Me, and I in him. As the living Father sent Me, and I live because of the Father, so he who eats Me, he also will live because of Me. This is the bread which came down out of heaven; not as the fathers ate and died; he who eats this bread will live forever."

Jesus is not talking about cannibalism here but about inner food, inner sustenance, upon which we are meant to live. We are to absorb Jesus, a metaphor for living on Jesus' body, soul, spirit, heart. The Scriptures say, "Have the mind of Christ." We are to absorb the mind, will, and emotions of Jesus. We are to absorb Jesus, absorb His motivations, and absorb His attitudes - just as our bodies absorb the bread and the wine when we partake of Christian communion. This is a ceremony when Christians remember Jesus' death and resurrection. We are to absorb Jesus' love and life into our spirits.

Jesus explains the process is analogous to his own relationship to the Father. He lived by feeding on the Father, and we are to live by feeding on Jesus. As He told His disciples in the upper room before His death through crucifixion,

"I in you and you in Me."

The 5,000 people whom Jesus miraculously fed bread and fish by the Lake of Galilee in Palestine, followed in the direction Jesus took the next day around the lake to find Him, because, as Jesus said to them, "You were fed and you want to eat some more."

Some of these people remind Jesus that Moses fed everyone in the wilderness with manna, a miraculous food, so now Jesus should feed everyone too, to prove He is just as great a prophet as Moses. Just think, no more work, no more scratching in the earth to grow food. Just give us food, they told Jesus, as Moses did, and we will make you king. Jesus reminds them that it was not Moses, but God, who gave the manna to their fathers.

After Jesus told them this, they said (John 6:35):

"Lord, give us this food." Jesus answers them: I am the bread of life; he who comes to Me will not hunger, and he who believes in Me will never thirst. But I said to you that you have seen Me, and yet do not believe. All that the Father gives Me will come to Me, and the one who comes to Me I will certainly not cast out. For I have come down from heaven, not to do My own will, but the will of Him who sent Me. This is the will of Him who sent Me, that of all that He has given Me I lose nothing, but raise it up on the last day. For this is the will of My Father, that everyone who beholds the Son and believes in Him will have eternal life, and I Myself will raise him up on the last day."

When these people heard what Jesus said, they started to grumble, "Yesterday He fed us, but today He is not going to give us anything to eat."

He says we must eat him! Come on, he is a man like us; we know his father and mother. How could He come down from heaven?

"Therefore the Jews were grumbling about Him, because He said, I am the bread that came down out of heaven. They were saying, is not this Jesus, the son of Joseph, whose father and mother we know? How does He now say, 'I have come down out of heaven'? Jesus answered and said to them, Do not grumble among yourselves. No one can come to Me unless the Father who sent Me draws him; and I will raise him up on the last day. It is written in the prophets, 'AND THEY SHALL ALL BE TAUGHT OF GOD.' Everyone who has heard and learned from the Father, comes to Me. Not that anyone has seen the Father, except the One who is from God; He has seen the Father.

Truly, truly, I say to you, he who believes has eternal life. I am the bread of life. Your fathers ate the manna in the wilderness, and they died. This is the bread which comes down out of heaven, so that one may eat of it and not die. I am the living bread that came down out of heaven; if anyone eats of this bread, he will live forever; and the bread also which I will give for the life of the world is My flesh."

After Jesus spoke these words, the people who heard Him started an argument, "How can we eat him? How can this man give us His flesh to eat?"

So Jesus said to them:

> "Truly, truly, I say to you, unless you eat the flesh of the Son of Man and drink His blood, you have no life in yourselves. He who eats My flesh and drinks My blood has eternal life, and I will raise him up on the last day. For My flesh is true food, and My blood is true drink. He who eats My flesh and drinks My blood abides in Me, and I in him. As the living Father sent Me, and I live because of the Father, so he who eats Me, he also will live because of Me. This is the bread which came down out of heaven; not as the fathers ate and died; he who eats this bread will live forever."

After those words, Jesus' disciples grumbled. Some disciples left and would not follow him anymore. The twelve, those who later became apostles, did not leave. The Apostle Peter said,

> "You, Jesus, are the Christ; You are the Holy One of God, the Son of the living God. You have words of eternal life."

Given these astounding statements of Jesus that He is indeed the spiritual food we Christians are to feed to our spirits, consider a little more understanding about our spirits

Our spirits are transcendent, not part of the created universe with its creation characteristics of time, space, matter, and energy. Our spirits are a thing of God given to make us persons. The Scriptures' basic principle is that God intended our spirits primarily to hold God's Spirit. But with the free agency God also gave to man, allowing sin, this intent has been corrupted so that man's spirits can also hold demonic powers.

The human spirit is like a cup meant to hold God's Spirit. In the records of the Old Testament, many accounts are given where a person is filled with the spirit of God and then enabled to carry out difficult tasks in the real world. Examples are King Saul, King David, Samson, Gideon, and others.

The spirit of wisdom was given to those who originally built the Mosaic Tabernacle in the wilderness after coming out of Egypt. The spirit of Moses was placed on the seventy elders who were to govern Israel with him. The Spirit of God came upon soothsayer Balaam when he was hired by the Moabites to curse the Hebrews but instead was moved by the Spirit to bless them. Joshua was filled with the spirit of wisdom when he was commissioned to conquer the land of Canaan.

The Spirit of the Lord came upon Othniel, son of Kenaz, as he judged Israel and went out to war. The Lord then gave Cushan-rishathaim, king of Mesopotamia, into his hand, and he prevailed over him.

According to Jeremiah the Prophet, the Lord stirred up the spirit of Cyrus, King of Persia, and he sent a proclamation throughout his entire kingdom, returning the Hebrews to Palestine. There are many examples like these where the Spirit of God moved into the spirit of a man, and motivated the man to do great things.

In the book of Job (32:8) it says:

> "But it is a spirit in man, the breath of the Almighty that gives him understanding."

Yes, that is it. The spirit of man gives him understanding.

Isaiah, (11:2) in the prophecy concerning the coming Messiah says:

> "The Spirit of the Lord will rest on Him,
> The spirit of wisdom and understanding,
> The spirit of counsel and strength,
> The spirit of knowledge and the fear of the LORD."

And (Joel 2:28):
> "It will come about after this:
> That I will pour out My Spirit on all mankind;
> And your sons and daughters will prophesy,
> Your old men will dream dreams,
> Your young men will see visions."

And in another place (Zechariah 12:1):

> "Thus declares the Lord who stretches out the heavens, lays the foundation of the earth, and forms the spirit of man within him"

(As a comment here, how could Zechariah possibly know that the "Inflationary Big Bang Theory" says that space was and is being stretched out, and now scientific observations have proved without doubt that space is still being continually stretched out? The accuracy and time invariant scope of the Old Testament Scriptures is simply astounding.)

And another, (Zechariah 12:10):

> "I will pour out on the house of David and on the inhabitants of Jerusalem, the spirit of grace and of supplication, so that they will look on Me whom they have pierced; and they will mourn for Him, as one mourns for an only son, and they will weep bitterly over Him like the bitter weeping over a firstborn."

Given these quotes, we can understand that God's Spirit moves into that of a man and can drive the man's being to do great tasks or give him spiritual insight or understanding and power to do great things.

The cup of the spirit concept implies that a man's spirit cup can accept other spirit input, so the spirit cup is partially filled by various spirits as the need arises.

In the New Testament Christian era, the Spirit of God also acts within mankind. In the book of 1ˢᵗ Corinthians (Chapter 12) we read:

> "Now there are varieties of gifts, but the same Spirit. And there are varieties of ministries, and the same Lord. There are varieties of effects, but the same God who works all things in all. But to each one is given the manifestation of the Spirit for the common good. For to one is given the word of wisdom through the Spirit, and to another the word of knowledge according to the same Spirit; to another faith by the same Spirit, and to another gifts of healing by the one Spirit, and to another the effecting of miracles, and to another prophecy, and to another the distinguishing of spirits, to another sundry kinds of tongues, and to another the interpretation of tongues. But one and the same Spirit works all these things, distributing to each one individually just as He wills."

Thus we have a little understanding of how God's Spirit interacts with man. Another quote (12:12-13):

> "For even as the body is one and has many members, and all the members of the body, though they are many, are one body, so also is Christ. For by one Spirit we were all baptized into one body, whether Jews or Greeks, whether slaves or free, and we were all made to drink of one Spirit."

And (1ˢᵗ Thessalonians 5:23-24):

"Now may the God of peace Himself sanctify you entirely; and may your spirit and soul and body be preserved complete, without blame at the coming of our Lord Jesus Christ. Faithful is He who calls you, and He also will bring it to pass."

One more quote (Galatians 5:19-25):

"Now the deeds of the flesh are evident, which are: immorality, impurity, sensuality, idolatry, sorcery, enmities, strife, jealousy, outbursts of anger, disputes, dissensions, factions, envying, drunkenness, carousing, and things like these, of which I forewarn you, just as I have forewarned you, that those who practice such things will not inherit the kingdom of God. But the fruit of the Spirit is love, joy, peace, patience, kindness, goodness, faithfulness, gentleness, self-control; against such things there is no law."

Christians are built by the power of Jesus Christ into a huge edifice of spiritual stones that make up the spiritual temple of God the Almighty. Jesus himself is the chief cornerstone of this temple (I Peter 2:4-8).

Realm of the Soul

By definition, the soul consists of the mind, the will, and the emotions. Over time perhaps the word soul has picked up other meanings but herein it has that definition. The soul is involved in cognitive processes or the result of cognitive process. Thinking, planning, the realm of imagining, calculating the results of some plan, creating images in one's mind – all of this is done in the realm of the soul. Business decisions, intellectual operations, government, making money, all that, is included and is part of the realm of the soul. Structures and systems that are in the world, but result from information, perhaps coded in the physical world, and yet are not of real physical substance in the world, are in the realm of the soul.

You might think of soul realm of life as one vast computer program. The program itself consists of words, statements, coding, or in your brain - molecules, electrical impulses, memory storage, and neuron connections. These physical elements are in the real world, the realm of the physical existence, but this computer program, when executed, generates results in the abstract which has meaning in itself, independent of the actual physical words, statements, or coding. The same thing occurs in the brain as part of the soul. All the molecules, electrical impulses, memory storage, and information coding in the brain generates a result in the abstract. This abstract does not consist of real physical entities, but concepts, so to speak, out in the ether.

The term ether (or aether) was created when physicists understood that in order for electromagnetic waves to propagate through space they needed a medium in which to travel. They called it, "ether", since they did not know what it was. Now that the Theory of Relativity has been discovered and verified, physicists understand ether is not required in order for electromagnetic waves to propagate, but the term is still useful, meaning we do not know what it is.

Abstract phenomenon is in the realm of the soul with its mind. You can dream, create something in the abstract, perhaps an image, but it exists only in your mind. This is life of the soul. This soul develops and grows, learns and matures as the rest of the body grows and matures.

There is a wonderful description of rational analysis and it is presented as wisdom in the Bible's book of Proverbs. The writer presents wisdom and understanding as a person, and describes God's use of wisdom/rational analysis in forming the universe. From Proverbs 8:22-31:

> The Lord possessed me at the beginning of His way,
> Before His works of old.
> From everlasting I was established,
> From the beginning, from the earliest times of the earth.
> When there were no depths I was brought forth,

> When there were no springs abounding with water,
> Before the mountains were settled,
> Before the hills I was brought forth;
> While He had not yet made the earth and the fields,
> Nor the first dust of the world.
>
> When He established the heavens I was there,
> When He inscribed a circle on the face of the deep,
> When he made firm the skies above,
> When the springs of the deep became fixed,
> When he set for the sea its boundary
> So that the water would not transgress His command,
> When He marked out the foundations of the earth.
>
> Then I was beside Him, a master workman;
> And I daily was His delight,
> Rejoicing always before Him,
> Rejoicing in the world, His earth,
> And my delight in the sons of men.

What a wonderful statement of the nature of the soul and its thinking process with its mind, will, and emotions. In these words of the Book of Proverbs, we come to understand that soul thinking existed before the physical universe was created, and that God used soul vision as an application of God's omnipotent understanding. God possessed this before anything physical existed.

Realm of the Body

This realm hardly needs a definition. All of observed creation is in this functional realm. This is the realm of the physical, the realm in which we dwell with our bodies. In the Bible this realm is often called flesh. This is the realm where we act out our lives. We can either do good, and do people good, or we can lie, cheat, and steal, and do evil. We either honor and keep our commitments, or we fornicate, and take advantage of people who come into our lives. In this realm we sin with acts of our bodies.

Most people think the flesh of the body is all there is of man's existence. As some unknown poet has said,

> "Into this world to eat and to sleep,
> And to know no reason why he was born,
> Save to consume the corn,
> Devour the cattle, flock and fish,
> And leave behind an empty dish."

Many theologians believe there are only two parts or two realms to mankind - the flesh of the visible world and the invisible world. The invisible world is undefined, but consists of everything invisible, including the soul, spirit, heart, and other terms in some impossible to fully understand imagery.

In the physical realm of the world of the flesh we suffer persecution and affliction. Sundry bad things happen to people and life can get very tough. God gets our attention when we fall into what some call a wilderness experience. For those maybe not familiar with the term, some examples of a wilderness experience might be when you lose all your lifetime accumulated assets, or when out of the blue your wife changes the locks on your home and files divorce papers, or when your husband says he is leaving for another woman, or when you suddenly develop an incurable disease, or when you are falsely accused of some crime and you are not able to defend yourself or prove your innocence. There are many other wilderness experiences, what the Bible calls trials and tribulations; some are not nearly as bad as those listed above, and some are worse.

God puts us in wilderness experiences where we seemingly cannot cope, in order to humble us so we may learn not to trust in our own resources, but to depend on God. The quickest way to become humble is to be thoroughly humiliated, which can happen more than a few times in one's life. Therefore, if you are a Christian, but you have lots of pride or pride rules in your life, wait a while; God will have you humiliated. God resists the proud but gives grace to the humble. If you need it, God will certainly humble you.

Summary of the Four Realms

I hope I have convinced you that you are a complex four-fold person, functioning in four realms as has been defined, as you have been made in the image of God. The scriptural evidence is overwhelming. Man functions in four realms. The primary thing in your life must be your heart. Deep down within your spirit is your heart, and it must love God. Your life in eternity depends on the love in your heart. Do you belong to God or not? That is the question.

There is clearly an enfolding relationship of the body to the soul to the spirit to the heart. A beautiful yet not readily understandable shadow picture of the relationship has been provided by God to us through the Bible. So come to understand now something of the Mosaic Tabernacle. This glorious picture of God dwelling among the Hebrews is a fantastic representation of the pre-incarnate Jesus Christ, but then also a representation of man. Jesus, of course, was a man.

Consider the Most Holy Place behind the inner curtain elaborate veil beyond the Holy Place where are the two gold cherubim, images of spiritual beings, indicating the spirit nature of the place. The Most Holy Place shadow pictures the realm of the spirit. In the tabernacle, the angel wings stood above the Ark of the Covenant. There was a small gap between the almost touching wings of the two cherubim above the Ark so the wings did not touch. From that gap, God told Moses, God would speak to Moses.

Here then is a shadow picture of your spirit; it, too, is of nothing, (meaning that the spirit is of no physical substance of the created universe) just like a gap would be, except for the air and space. But the gap between angel wings, a representation of your spirit, overshadows an ark. This gap between the wings of your guardian angels is where your spirit, given to you by God, has a dwelling place, and communicates to your heart and your soul.

There was a curtain separating the Hebrew Tabernacle spirit inner room from the soul room; this was before Jesus came on the earth. The curtain then indicated filtered communication between the spirit and the soul, sometimes open and sometimes closed, sometimes with light from the lamp and sometimes not.

In the room of the soul, as represented by the Holy Place in the Tabernacle, is continual mental food for knowledge, indicated by the table of shew bread, continual mental light to guide the path in life as indicated by the lamp, and daily mental communication through prayer to God, as indicated by the censer for incense smoke on its altar.

Then there is a curtain separating your soul room from the real physical world outside where you are washed in regeneration in preparation for worship, and a sacrifice has been made to God on your behalf – the precious life, body, and blood of your Savior, Jesus Christ.

What a beautiful picture of human life as it relates to God, and how your worship and knowledge of God is conducted and manifested.

In the days of Hebrew tabernacle and temple use, the priest went daily into the Holy Place to put in order the bread, replenish the lamp olive oil, and replenish the especially formulated incense resin oil for the incense censer. Once a year the High Priest, opened the curtain to the Holy of Holies, took a censor full of burning coals from the altar, and generated incense smoke from two handfuls of finely ground fragrant incense. Taking a bowl of blood from the sacrifice with him, his way lighted by the lamp, the High Priest sprinkled the Ark with blood from the animal sacrifice. The Book of Hebrews in the Christian New Testament of the Bible explains this picture.

The Book of Hebrews tells us the tabernacle Moses built is a representation of a tabernacle in Heaven, in the eternities. In the Tabernacle of the Eternities, the High Priest, Jesus Christ, our Savior, once for all appeared and presented his own blood in the Heavenly Holy of Holies, and passed through the heavens, having sacrificed Himself for the forgiveness of the sins of his chosen ones. The book says that is why the Old Testament Hebrew High Priest appeared only once a year in the inner room - the Holy of Holies, the Holy Spirit of God showing by this that the way into the Heavenly Holy of Holies was not yet open while the Old Testament Tabernacle/Temple was still standing or had standing (In the metaphysical sense). Before Jesus was crucified the curtain veil separated the spirit room from the soul room.

When the crucifixion of our Lord Jesus was finished, and Jesus died on that cross, the earth shook, and the veil of the Temple in Jerusalem was torn in two from top to bottom, signifying the Christian's room of the soul is now open to the Christian's room of the spirit with unfiltered communication as indicated by this veil rendering. Now there is open access to the inner essence being, our hearts, into the Heavenly Holy of Holies in the eternities.

How wonderful now is also the presence of the Holy Spirit of God as It abides in the room of the Christian's spirit, to comfort, guide, witness, and so also then to feed the soul with truth through direct access to the believing soul.

Now that Moses' earthly tabernacle and subsequent Hebrew temples have been destroyed, by wars with Philistines, Babylonians, and Romans, Jesus appeared on earth and eternally once offered his blood of the New Covenant in the Holy of Holies of the eternities, we believers in His Name are washed clean with regeneration, forgiven of all our sins, and made perfect before God. We now belong to our faithful Savior Jesus Christ, and there is open access to our inner being, our heart, into the Heavenly Holy of Holies in the eternities.

Stupendously astounding! Praise God! Praise you, Jesus!

What an amazing picture. Jesus, a man just like us, yet fully God, God in the flesh, has become our high priest, knowing all our weaknesses, has ascended, passed through the eternal Holy of Holies in the heavens, and sprinkled his own eternal life-giving blood on each of our hearts to make us perfect before God.

To sum up, understand now that God supremely rules in all of the four realms. From the imagery of the Apostle John in the Book of Revelation we receive a marvelous picture. The four creatures covered all over with eyes surrounding the Throne of God and the Lamb, tell us that God observes everything, and rules in everything, and His rule is supreme and operates in these four realms. Not only does God supremely rule over His physical creation, He supremely rules in the thoughts and aspirations of man, and in all the imaginations of man. God's rule is supreme in the spirit realm over all spirits, and God's rule is supreme in the hearts of all mankind.

But given all this, in His supreme sovereignty God, nevertheless, has allowed Satan to become the god of this age (II Corinthians 4:4), ruler of the kingdom of the air (Ephesians 2:2), and now has the power of death (Hebrews 2:14).

This supreme rule of God is a very vast concept. Most of mankind dwell in serene nothing and are absolutely ignorant of God, and most could care less. Nevertheless, God rules and is supremely supreme.

FIVE

Peter's Four-fold Steps

Peter, the leader of Jesus' apostles, wrote the Second Epistle of Peter in the Bible, telling us what to do with the faith we have been given (II Peter 1:3-4).

"Grace and peace be multiplied to you in the knowledge of God and of Jesus our Lord; seeing that His divine power has granted to us everything pertaining to life and godliness, through the true knowledge of Him who called us by His own glory and excellence. For by these He has granted to us His precious and magnificent promises, so that by them you may become partakers of divine nature, having escaped the corruption that is in the world by lust."

God's divine power has given us everything we need for life and godliness through knowledge. Yes, through the promises of God we may participate in the divine nature and escape corruption.

Consider now the fourfold four realm application of Peter's imperatives that we are to diligently pursue.

Fourth Realm: Faith

Faith begins and develops in your fourth realm, the life within your inner essence of your heart. Your inner self, your heart, by the prompting of the Spirit of God, tells you God is real; although you do not completely understand, God's love overshadows you, and you start to know that God is seeking fellowship with you. You respond and you believe.

Second Realm: Virtue, Knowledge, Self-control

Peter describes a progression of qualities to be added to your faith and says to pursue them diligently. He says to be diligent. First add moral virtue to your faith. God is revealing Himself to you, and

God is the God of love and truth. God wants you to be morally good because God is morally good. You may be in the depth of moral degradation, full of sin and disgusted with yourself, or maybe you have lived such a life of sin it is hard to know what moral virtue is. It does not matter into what depth of sin you have fallen. You must adopt mental imperatives and then hear or read and understand God's law and His moral goodness, and resolve within yourself to reject sin and live a morally good life.

You repent of any and all sin. You do this in your mind. Carrying out this mental commitment to moral virtue in the real world sometimes is very difficult, but do not give up regardless of your ongoing mistakes. God will gently help you regardless of your past. Carrying out this mental commitment happens in the second realm, the life of the soul, which includes the mind, will, and emotions. You decide in your mind to be committed to moral virtue.

All sin begins in the mind. You see a woman and lust after her, or you have envy and desire some other woman's husband to look after you and take care of you. Maybe you observe some wealth or property and you want it. Sometimes you may be seized with anger and want to harm someone severely. Perhaps someone has done you wrong, and you think he or she needs chastising. All this occurs in your soul, the mind, will, and emotions in your second realm. Therefore, your soul needs to take control and put a stop to such wrong thinking. This is the process of adding moral virtue to your life; it is done in your mind. Peter says to do that diligently.

Peter says the next thing to do is to add knowledge to your moral virtue. That is to study or try to understand God's laws and the nature of God, and how God interacts with man. Knowledge includes understanding God's purpose for your life. Study how God interacts with people and instructs them. Our primary source of knowledge about God is the Bible and God's magnificently created universe. Sincere Christian brothers and sisters, pastors and priests are also a source of knowledge and understanding. In our age there are books without end, some good and some bad. Knowledge, like moral virtue, occurs in the soul, your second realm. Wisdom is a product of knowledge, applying knowledge to live life skillfully.

Peter then says to add self-control to your knowledge. Self-control essentially means that your mind controls what you do. When you are provoked or disturbed by some event, you do not respond with anger leading to rage, or envy, or verbally or physically damaging someone. This is true with children, especially. Children can be quite damaged by thoughtless words or blows that are undeserved. Self-control means your mind takes over your emotions after a short interval, so you do not let yourself sin in your anger or envy. Self-control takes place in the soul, in your third realm.

First Realm: Perseverance, Godliness, Kindness

Peter next says to diligently add perseverance to your self-control. Perseverance is to be consistent in your responses, to act steadily in the real physical world. This occurs in the first realm, life in the real physical world, the realm of life in the body of flesh. Perseverance means to go ahead steadily and practice your Christian life consistently. Practice moral virtue, accumulation of knowledge, and self-control consistently, to have a consistent response in the real world, the world of the first realm.

Peter says to add godliness to your perseverance and do it diligently. Godliness means to act in this world the way God would act. Godliness means to take on the character of God. Study Jesus' responses to events or words in His life, how He interacted with people – there is your example of godliness.

The last of the first realm real-world attributes which Peter says to add diligently to godliness is brotherly kindness. That does not really need any explaining. Brotherly kindness is really just kindness to anyone in the world, but in a very special sense to your Christian brothers and sisters. Being kind to unlovable people or those difficult to love is sometimes very hard. Yet Christians are called upon by God, here through these words of Peter, to be kind, especially to fellow Christians.

Kindness makes for a happy life. Treating other people with kindness usually results in their treating you with kindness. When we are treated with kindness and respect, it seems to create within us a sense of self-worth feeding our happiness. Yes, treat everyone with kindness so they are encouraged in their Christian faith. Unbelievers may observe your kindness and be attracted to it, seeking to find the reason for your kindness, discover you are a Christian, and then seek to become a Christian themselves.

Third Realm: Love

The last of Peter's progression is love. Peter says to diligently add love to brotherly kindness. The love Peter is talking about occurs in the third realm, our life with God in our spirits. This is the life in our spiritual being. When our hearts, our most inner essence being in our fourth realm, belong to Jesus, God's Spirit comes and makes his home within our spirit. We respond with love of God. We are commanded by God to love God with all our heart, spirit, soul, and strength, and our neighbor as our self. God is love. We are to live with God in love, love here in this life, and love throughout eternity. This means that the third realm love in our spirits is to dominate our whole being, permeating out to our souls, and then into our physical life of real action in the real world.

When this, our fourth realm loving heart, dominates our life and especially our life with God, we are filled with love. The fourth realm heart life then dominates the third realm spirit life and fills our second realm soul with love. Our attitudes and motivations within our spirits, fed from our hearts, reflect love. Our minds, wills, and emotions reflect love. With our souls in control of our bodies, we act with love in the real world of the first realm, doing deeds of love and kindness in our physical life on the Earth.

As a little further application of the realm understanding, consider more of our third realm, our spirits. In the spirit realm mending and healing of our brokenness occurs. Christians are built by the power of Jesus Christ into a huge edifice of spiritual stones that make up the spiritual temple of God the Almighty. Jesus himself is the chief cornerstone of this temple.

What decision will you make? Are you feeding on Jesus, assimilating Jesus? Do all the realms of your life, your life's multiple functions, seek to absorb Jesus? Do you try to live your life in the flesh as Jesus would? Do you try to think good thoughts and dream good dreams, as Jesus would? Do you examine your attitudes and motivations to see if they are assimilating Jesus' attitudes and motivations?

Jesus has promised the Holy Spirit to those who ask. By far, the most important step in assimilating Jesus is to ask God for the life of Jesus to come into you. Ask Him to send His Holy Spirit so It may come into your spirit and witness to your spirit. Ask Him to feed your four functional realms being with His life. He will not deny you. The Holy Spirit will live in you and work on you from the inside out.

Now that I have given you the realm concept as applied by Peter with application from the spirit, the goal is to achieve love in all of our life, in our foursome functional existence, in all our four realm existence.

SIX

Apostolic Realm Ministries

Ray Stedman in his most excellent book on 1st John[2] referred to the ideas of Watchman Nee[1], concerning the different stages of emphasis in the ministries into which the several apostles were called. Jesus called Peter while he was fishing. Jesus gave to Peter the ministry of fishing for men (Mathew 4:19). Jesus called the apostle John while he and his brother James were mending the fishing nets of their father Zebedee. Subsequently, John has a mending ministry (Matthew 4:21-22).

Jesus, after His resurrection from the dead, spoke with a powerful voice from the heavens to encounter the Apostle Paul (then called Saul) when he was on the road to Damascus where Saul intended to persecute the followers of Jesus (Acts 9:3-6). Paul had the skills of a maker of tents, a builder of tents. Paul's ministry became one of laying foundations and building the Christian Church.

Jude, in the little book of Jude warns about false prophets and false teachers. Jude identifies himself as the brother of James. James, not the same James as the brother of John identified above who King Herod killed, was a leader of the early Church. Jude was called to a ministry of identifying false teachers, false ministers, and false prophets.

In this calling of four apostles for ministries, there is a pattern so that we have again a four realm four-fold theme. These four emphases of ministry are basic to the formation of the early church and they do indeed have a four-fold operational nature. This four-fold ministry operation is essential for the ultimate, very marvelous, very astounding, wonderful development, and success of the early Christian Church.

Also, as a complete, not so obvious parallel to this, there is a four-fold realm manifestation of growth in each human individual encounter with the Lord Jesus and His gospel, and in so doing, creating a complete mature Christian.

Peter's Ministry of Catching Men

First consider Peter's ministry. Peter was called to a ministry to catch and gather many of those of man into the Kingdom of God. Peter is the leader of the early church and is to go out and win people for the cause of Jesus Christ, to establish the Church. Peter preaches in Jerusalem and 5,000 people respond and become believers. The development of the Church begins under Peter's leadership.

Peter, subsequently, is called to go out to the gentiles and bring them into the Kingdom of Jesus Christ. Peter has the vision from God of the sheet full of various animals descending from heaven. In that vision God declares all foods clean and so sets aside the Jewish law. Peter leads out in the direction which the Church is to follow. Peter is the first leader of the Church. Peter begins the Church.

When a person comes to know the Lord Jesus as his Savior and Lord, the Holy Spirit washes and purifies that person's heart, an operation in the fourth realm, that of the heart (Acts 15:9). Peter's ministry of catching men and women and bringing them into the vast Kingdom of God has a parallel to the beginning in each individual person's walk with the Lord. The first step into the Kingdom for each individual person, and also the first operation for building the Lord's universal Church, are similar first step operations. Through Peter's style of ministry preaching with reaching out to unbelievers, many believers are incorporated into the one body, the universal Church. This, of course is what happened in Jerusalem where the Church began.

Paul's Ministry of Church Building

After a time, the Church in Jerusalem is persecuted. A most aggressive persecutor is a man named Saul. On the road to Damascus, where Saul intended to persecute believers, Jesus appears to him, puts a stop to his persecutions, and gives Saul, later to be called Paul, a ministry in the Kingdom. Paul had a skill, as each Jewish boy was required to have a skill, of a tent maker/builder. Paul was called when he was a tent maker, that is, one who builds or makes things. So Paul is called to a ministry to be a builder of the Universal Church of Jesus Christ.

Paul, subsequently, meets directly with Jesus out in real physical desert wilderness, and Jesus directly teaches him. Jesus then sends him out into the existential wilderness for a while, to wander and grow in spirit and soul, and spends time alone reflecting on his knowledge of Jesus, and come to understand who Jesus really is.

After the beginning of the Church, perhaps about 20 years later, Paul begins to execute and perform his astounding ministry of evangelism, of teaching people, of writing down theology, of laying foundations, and of building up the Church of the Lord Jesus. Paul preaches and then writes down basic theology, knowledge about many things beneficial to the Church, teachings, and understanding for the Kingdom of God. Understanding and knowledge of the Kingdom occur in the second realm, that of the soul.

This second realm operation starts to occur in the historical Church maybe about twenty years after the church had its beginning. For the first twenty years after Jesus rose from the dead, Peter's style and emphasis of ministry beginning prevailed. After 20 years the style and ministry of Paul became more dominate in the universal Church. Similarly, in each individual person's Christian life, after the heart has been washed and purified in a fourth realm operation, understanding, building, and development of the Christian life, through study and absorbing of knowledge occur. This is through an operation in the second realm, that of the soul.

Jude's Ministry Dealing with False Prophets

The ministry of Jude dealing with false prophets at first seems a little strange. Jesus tells us that by their fruits you will know them. Thus in our Christian lives as we go forth and encounter the trials and tribulations of life and fellowship with other believers in the Church, along come encounters with false teachers, those who preach another gospel.

The historical record shows that in 70 AD, about 40 years after the crucifixion of Jesus, and about 20 years after the initiation of Paul's ministry of Christian teaching, theology, and understanding, the Roman armies come and destroy Jerusalem and the Temple of the Jews. This, of course, destroyed the Jewish homeland and dispersed the Jews all over the known world and terminated Temple worship. Jewish Christians in the homeland of the Jews were also scattered all over the known world. What a terrible trial and tribulation.

Josephus, the Jewish Roman historian[3], indicates approximately a million Jews died in the fighting, about a million were sold into slavery, and about a million were scattered abroad. Some, especially the Christians, left before the Romans did their thing. Jesus had warned, while imparting prophecy to his followers, when you see Jerusalem surrounded by armies, leave. After Jerusalem was destroyed, it seems, there was a great occasion for the introduction of heresy and false teaching throughout the Church. The Book of Jude, which severely warns against false teachers, was written in this period.

False teaching of another gospel is hard to intellectually recognize. The words of false teachers are smooth and seem correct, so discernment sometimes is difficult. But Jesus tells us,

"By their fruits you will know them."

Fruits occur in the realm of the flesh, the first realm of the body in physical creation. Thus when you observe teachers, preachers and priests indulging in fornication, homosexual practice, adultery, theft, covetousness, pursuit of lucre, and such, then you know what they have been preaching and teaching is false!

Yes, false teachers fall by works of the flesh. Flesh is in the first realm, that of the body, in the real physical world. False teachers can preach wonderfully. They can craft great theology and helps marvelously, and even preach so as to bring people into the Kingdom. I have known people who have come to know the Lord Jesus while even in a cult! They were under false teaching, but reading the Bible and praying opened their heart eyes to belief and then to be saved and have their hearts washed and purified. Somewhere along the way, of course, they discover the truth and abandon the false teacher or false Church denomination.

Eventually, each cult and other false teachers within the Church demonstrate evil practice in the flesh. Yes, even false church denominations get discovered by works of corruption. The practice of homosexual activity, adultery, fornication, and the tolerance of such in a Church clearly demonstrate that Church to be false. So called gay marriage or gay leadership in a Church demonstrates that assembly to be false. "By their fruits you will know them."

All these corrupt activities occur in the realm of the flesh, the first realm. So observe the sins of the body of flesh and be warned. In the historical Church it seems that Jude preached and wrote his epistle sometime after 70 AD when Jerusalem and the temple were destroyed. However, in the life of the individual person of man, it seems that false teachers can show up any time in the Christian's life development of knowledge and understanding, especially, when the believer is going through a trial or tribulation.

John's Ministry of Spiritual Mending

Perhaps 40 years after the start of the Apostle Paul's ministry or after about 90 AD, 20 years after the destruction of Jerusalem, the Apostle John writes the books attributed to him in the Bible. John was called while he was mending the fishing nets of his father, and we understand from John's books that John's emphasis is on mending and healing in the Christian life, with tremendous emphases on spiritual growth of the believer.

In our Christian life we too are called, we then believe, and our hearts are washed and purified by the Spirit of God; we live out our life in the body. We read and hear and understand about the kingdom, Gods purposes and plans, but then as the trials, troubles, vicissitudes, and tribulations of life descend onto us, we need healing, mending, and spiritual development. We need to constantly put our Christian life back together as we become convoluted with temptations, tragedies, trials, troubles, backslides, what not's, and also attempt to ferret out false teaching from pastors, priests, and other would-be Christian leaders.

That is also what happened to the early Church. The Church was persecuted. Many attempts were made to destroy the Church. After the Romans came and destroyed Jerusalem, the Church was scattered all over the Roman Empire - then came an era of false teaching and apostasy. Many wondered, "What is going on?" John's healing ministry of mending and spiritual development gave new confidence in the power of the gospel of Jesus Christ. John's ministry mended the Church and gave it a tremendous new beginning among the gentiles. The Church of Jesus Christ then expanded all over the known world in a very astounding process. Mending and healing occur in the third realm, that of spirit.

What a composite glorious picture of the God-directed beginning and early development of the Church of Jesus Christ! 20 years of Peter's emphasis on beginnings, 20 years of Paul's emphasis on knowledge and understanding, 20 years of emphasis on defeating false teaching through the instructions of Jude (as Jude so powerfully condemns it), and then years of John's ministry's emphasis of healing, mending, and spiritual growth, which have continued throughout the complete continuing development of the Church.

The universal Church, having a complete four-fold mandate of the Gospel of Jesus Christ, was ready to go out and conquer the world for Jesus' Kingdom and has continued to do so for the last almost 2,000 years.

A number, when supplied in the Bible, has in the number itself often a very important significant message --- perhaps indicating an overall event. The number unit the Bible indicates is a much more significant meaning than any reference to an actual count contained by such a number. We occidentals consider numbers to have exact meaning, such as a dozen eggs being exactly twelve eggs. This is not necessarily true for the Bible which tends to have an oriental view of things. Forty, for example, seems to have much more an extended meaning than an actual exact count of forty items. For example, the Hebrews wandered 40 years in the wilderness, King David reigned for 40 years in Jerusalem; Jesus was tempted by the devil for 40 days. The list of number of events using 40 is huge. Forty seems to mean a period of trial or testing. The meaning of the trial or testing event is more important that any actual count of forty.

Peter's initial style of beginning ministry lasted one-half of a 40-year period of trial; Paul's initial style of teaching ministry lasted one-half period of a 40-year trial. Jerusalem was destroyed after a 40-year period of trial by the Jews. With no repentance and no grieving over the One they had pierced - the Romans came.

After the Romans did their thing, there was a one-half of a 40-year period of emphasis on false prophets and false teaching in the ministry of the Church. Then come the writings of the Apostle John. John's style of ministry occurs where healing and mending become an emphasis in the ministry of the Church. Healing and mending of Christians believers then continued, and continues on today in the Church until that day when Jesus comes again and we have the end of the Church on earth, and we have a new heaven and a new earth.

The historical time sequence of early Church development is quite fascinating. Peter was crucified, upside down according to tradition, about 33 years after Jesus' crucifixion or about 63 AD. Peter probably had spent some time in a Roman prison so Peter's ministry had been terminated before this. Paul was beheaded about 68 AD, and so his ministry was terminated. Jerusalem was destroyed in 70 AD. Jude was executed at the beginning of the reign of the Roman Emperor Trajan, about 98 AD, his ministry against false teachers was also then terminated.

It is very interesting that when Jesus gave the commands to Peter (John 21:15-22) to "Tend My lambs," "Shepherd my sheep," "Tend my sheep," after Jesus resurrection from the dead, at the barbeque fish breakfast on the seashore, and predicted to Peter his death by crucifixion, Peter then asked Jesus, "How about John?" John was walking behind Jesus and Peter, and Jesus said, "If I want him to remain until I come, what is that to you? You follow Me!"

So John continued to live on earth after Jude's execution, perhaps even until about 117 AD, and apparently died of natural causes. Historians have not established a reliable estimate of the date.

Understand another very significant number message. When Peter puled in the net with a huge haul of fish, some for the barbeque breakfast, the account says they caught 153 large fish. What? How many people count the exact number of fish they caught after mentally counting the first dozen? Again the number 153 must be very profound and important. Why does the Bible book of John when describing a fellowship breakfast meal with the resurrected Jesus, an astounding all-consuming event, record that 153 fish were caught in the net?

Factoring that 153 number we obtain ten plus seven, times three squared. Wow! Indeed! Seven is the covenant number, the oath number, the number of days in a week, and ten is the completeness number, the everybody included number, the everything number, and three is the fulfilment number! Jesus was three days in the tomb. So interpreting the meaning of the number 153 we have the covenant relationship plus the entire completeness of everything, the total sum multiplied by the fulfillment number squared. Yes, Jesus is saying, everything has been accomplished! Indeed! Now go out and gather in my lambs and build my Church.

To sum up and establish in your mind the astounding success of Jesus' ministry on earth, John's book, chapter 21, gives us the very clear message indicating Jesus has accomplished all that the Father gave Him to do.

These terminations of the several apostles' respective ministries are very fascinating to me as God raises up another style of ministry after the forces of evil terminate a ministry. The Church grows and marvelously further develops with each sequential ministry. All this demonstrates God is in control and is supremely omnipotent. The Holy Spirit of Jesus develops His Church no matter what forces its enemies put forth.

In parallel to these phenomena in the universal church, so it is in our own individual Christian life. Each believer has a beginning by being washed and purified by the Holy Spirit within. This is a fourth realm heart operation. Then believers grow in knowledge and understanding in their minds within their second realm of soul. Then they face the trials, tribulations, temptations of the world, living out life in their flesh, in the first realm of their body, in the real physical world. Then mending, healing, and spiritual growth occur through their third realm, that of spirit, while the Holy Spirit lives within their spirit. Consequently, they come to intensively love Jesus, and love Him very deeply, indeed.

Yes, this is the sequential progression of the Christian life leading to maturity.

There is another very interesting profound occurrence that sometimes happens in the Christian person's life. After a time in the first two realms in the Kingdom, the period of the beginning of the Christian life like in Peter's ministry, and then a period of intellectual soul growth like in Paul's ministry, the Christian is presented with a Jerusalem event.

The Christian's life is developing; he or she has a wife or husband, wonderful home and children, and is living out the Christian life in prosperity and seemingly all goodness. Then something happens; let's call it a Jerusalem event. Life seems to be destroyed. All of the accumulated life assets are lost, the spouse gets incurable cancer and dies, an automobile accident takes away spouse or children, spouse decides to have a midlife crisis and abandons you and the children - a Jerusalem event - where everything is seemingly lost. Is God in control or not? Does God love me, or does He not love me?

The 40-year-like testing period of beginning and soul growth symbolized by the number 40, wherein an initial trial of God has now taken place - the beginning and soul growing in the Lord period is complete. God then in the very strange enigma of life, in His most omnipotent way, works about a substantial trial to prove to Satan this Christian really does belong to Him. Yes, a Job-like trial happens! Ow! It hurts!

So consider then the lessons from the Bible book of Job. Job has everything and serves God in everything, and Satan tells God, "Sure Job serves You because You protect him. Take away everything he has and he will curse You." Well, Job loses everything and still loves God. Then Satan says, "Take away his health and his friends and then he will curse You." God permits Satan to do his thing.

So Jobs health is destroyed and some awful "comforter" friends arrive to mentally torment him. Job is sitting on an ash heap scratching himself with a potsherd to relieve a little of the misery, and Job's wife comes along and tells him, "Job! Haven't you had enough? Curse God and die!"

Yes, in your abject pain and misery of your trial, will you just curse God and die, and so prove Satan correct? Yes, life sometimes has an awful event that is a really a terrible ugly trial. Will you come to the point where you will accept Job's wife's advice and curse God and die?

In some strange way, almost impossible for man to understand, God wants the very loving marvelous Christian person to become an even better, yet even more marvelous Christian, an even more loving understanding person. So along comes a Jerusalem event - a terrible, terrible trial.

But in all of this your trial, remember Jesus loves you; Jesus' love is the answer to everything.

Remember now, like the early Universal Church, for full Christian life development, you have two more realms to go! You are ready and have the power to fight false teachers, fight the corruption of mankind, and fight the corrupt civilization around you, and yes, you now have the power to get rid of all the stupid sin in your life!

Through your suffering you will now receive true discernment to recognize false teachers, false prophets, and false brethren. You will now receive spiritual gifts from the Holy Spirit of God. You will now understand Jude's ministry of condemnation of false teaching, and the Apostle John's ministry of spiritual growth, mending and healing! You can now be very productive in the Kingdom of Jesus Christ on earth. You will now be able to comfort those God brings into your life, those who need help, comfort, healing, and mending. You can confidently look forward to full wonderful eternal life with Jesus. Praise God!

Then there is fantastic blessing. Consider again Job and the result of all his suffering. In Job's case God restored his prosperity. But the most fantastic thing is the names Job gave to his daughters in his new second family of seven sons and three daughters. Translation is always a bit tricky, but Pastor Ray Stedman suggests the translated names to be Peace, Fragrance, and Beauty.

Yes, indeed! The names Job gave to his daughters reflected what happened in and to his life! So for you, too, your result, the fruit of your awful suffering, projected marvelously into your life, healed and mended, now with the deep love of Jesus in your heart, on earth and on into eternity, similar to Job, is a marvelous Christian life of peace, fragrance, and beauty!

Peace is a state of the mind, will, and emotions - a possession and manifestation of the soul. So Job and you, after all your trials and tribulations have a life of peace in your soul!

Beauty is a glow and condition of the spirit. Other believers see the beauty of your spirit and rejoice!

Fragrance is an aroma pleasing to God. As the Apostle Paul writes in II Corinthians 2:15-16,

> "We are a fragrance of Christ to God among those being saved and among those who are perishing; to the one an aroma from death to death, to the other an aroma of life to life."

Indeed, including the realm of the body, here is another four-fold realm manifestation.

And now, yes! With great joy, enjoy your very loving Christian life of peace, fragrance, and beauty.

SEVEN

Fruitful Man, Spirit, Fornication

From the book of Genesis chapter nine (1-7), after the account of the flood which destroyed all of man except for Noah and his family, we read:

"And God blessed Noah and his sons and said to them, "Be fruitful and multiply and fill the earth. The fear of you and the terror of you will be on every beast of the earth and on every bird of the sky; with everything that creeps on the ground, and all fish of the sea, into your hands they are given.

Every moving thing that is alive shall be food for you; I give all to you, as the green plant. Only you shall not eat flesh with its life, its blood. Surely I will require your lifeblood, from every beast I will require it. And from every man, from every man's brother I will require the life of man.

Whoever sheds man's blood,
By man his blood shall be shed,
For in the image of God,
He made man.

As for you be fruitful and multiply; populate the earth abundantly and multiply in it."

Yes, the command of God given to our forefather Noah is to be fruitful and multiply in the earth! This command is completely contrary to the present thinking of the intelligentsia of the western nations. Many modern deluded men want to terminate the growth of the human race. Undoubtedly, this is the work of Satan, the great enemy of God. Satan seeks death for as many of man as possible and certainly wants to prevent as many new believing people for God on the earth as possible. Satan wants to exterminate as many little humans as possible through the abortion process.

God was very angry with those of the Hebrew people who offered their children by fire to the fire god Moloch.   Modern incineration of little humans bodies after abortion is very little different. Young lives are terminated as an offering to Satan. Wow! What evil!

One wonders, "What is going on? Why all this evil? What is God's overall purpose?"   God is searching man for fellowship – countless multitudes of them. But God gives free will, too; man can choose corruption and set his course to hate and despise God. In the end of all things, of course, those who hate or despise God are destroyed.

The nature and supreme attribute of God is righteousness. God is good and He desires fellowship with man, male and female, who are good. So goodness and righteousness is the imperative God gives to man. The whole Christian gospel is the process of God is making righteous men and women out of this race of wicked man who are corrupt and deserve death, and should be destroyed. The true Christian gospel is all about the process of how each of man is to become saved and become a righteous sinner.

Multiply and Fill the Earth

Here are the commands and imperatives from the text:

Multiply and fill the earth abundantly
Rule over everything
Everything alive is food, but not the blood
Must kill every man murderer, either man or beast,
     Because man is made in image of God

Astoundingly, here again is a set of four realm imperative commands given to man. To rule is symbolized by the lion and to rule is the imperative given to man.

"You shall rule over everything."

Ruling is a fourth realm operation, that of heart.

Every murderer of man shall in turn, be killed.   Man is composed with a spirit in the image of God so God commands that anyone who murders man must in turn be deprived of life and put to death.   The spiritual ramifications of this indicate this is to be a third realm operation, that of spirit, because man is made in the image of God.

From the Scriptures (I Corinthians 3:16-17):

> "You are a temple of God and the Spirit of God dwells in you. If any man destroys the temple of God, God will destroy him, for the temple of God is holy, and that is what you are."

We must take this as a very serious warning.

The initial scripture of this also said, multiply, fill the earth, create civilizations – this is an operation in the second realm, that of planning to do things, the realm of the soul.

Of course, to eat to sustain life is in the realm of the flesh, that of the body, the first realm.   Man may use as food anything that has life - animals and plants.   But man must not eat the blood.   God says life is in the blood and, therefore, must not be eaten.

This is a very interesting command.   It makes one stop and think. What is so important about the blood?   Scientifically, the blood carries oxygen to all parts of the body - to each living cell.   Oxygen is part of the air, a symbol of the spirit, as God breathes the breath of life into man to give them life as a being.   Therefore, God has commanded man not to eat or assimilate the lifeblood, as symbolized for the spirit of animals. This is certainly a very curious thing which cannot be known by scientific study.   Perhaps animals have spirits which must not be assimilated into man.

In the book of Acts Chapter 28 is an account of the Apostle Paul spending a full day preaching in the city of Rome to an assembly of Jews and Romans.   After the day of preaching and teaching some believed in the Lord Jesus Christ and some did not.   When he finished,

Paul spoke a parting word to them, directed at the unbelieving Jews, quoting the Prophet Isaiah, saying, the Holy Spirit spoke rightly to your fathers. Paul spoke as follows (Acts 28:26-27):

> "Go to this people and say,
>> You will keep on hearing, but will not understand;
>> And you will keep on seeing, but will not perceive;
>> For the heart of this people has become dull,
>> And with their ears they scarcely hear,
>> And they have closed their eyes;
>> Otherwise they might see with their eyes,
>> And hear with their ears,
>> And understand with their hearts and return,
>> And I would heal them."

Eyes are a symbol of spirit. Hearing is a function of the soul. Understanding is a thing of the heart. Yes, including the realm of the flesh, this is another four realm statement.

What an astounding statement of how man stands before God and can either be healed of all his weaknesses and corruption, or be left in his ugly, awful, depraved, unhealed state. Yes, man perceives with his spirit, hears with his soul, and understands with the heart.

Man a Four Realm Person

Why does God make it a four realm operation? That is a very profound question. It is the result of the way God has made man. It is the way we are. It is the way the universe is! Understand the difference because it is the difference between life eternal and eternal death. You are a four-fold four-realm person. There are functional distinctions between your soul, your spirit, and your heart. They are not the same thing, or part of the same thing.

Many theologians have preached and taught that man is composed of the visible and the invisible, that is, body and soul, where they define soul to be everything invisible. Many other theologians have preached that man is composed of body, soul, and spirit. This is certainly more correct. I sincerely hope that you have come to understand that the invisible part of man is composed of heart, spirit, and soul. The difference is important for you to understand, so as to understand yourself, and to understand a little more about God.

It is important to know the condition of the heart is the defining difference between life and death. The difference is binary. That is, either you belong to Jesus Christ or you do not. Yes or no. Yes, this is binary, either one or zero. Your heart is either washed and purified or it is not washed and purified. Understand that!

Once your heart is washed and purified and you summit to Jesus, the Holy Spirit begins a work in your life. You have been justified (Given right standing with God) and now begins the work of being sanctified (Growing in the process of becoming Christ like). You must let the Holy Spirit work. This, again, is a profound thing. The Holy Spirit is very, very patient, yet sin against the Holy Spirit leads to death and is not forgiven.

God hates sin. Creating rules to follow and claiming that righteousness consists of following these rules is great error. The Holy Spirit within you, using God's Word, the Bible, will help direct your life so you know what to do and what not to do in the choices you make. Your motivation must be love; first love of God and then love of your fellow man.

Love does not do wrong, evil things. Let love be your motivation as the choices of life are made. Love does not abandon wife or children for a hot slut, or seek pleasure of the flesh for a season, or when the first covenant love of your life is abandoned.

Judaizers in the Early Church

In the early church were Judaizers, those who came up from Jerusalem to the Asia Minor area and told the new gentile Christian believers there they must follow the Jewish law and be circumcised. (Yes, there are some today who still advocate that following the law leads to righteousness --- a great error) This troubled the Church so the Apostle Paul and Barnabas went from there to Jerusalem to lay the problem before the apostles and leaders of the Church. After much debate James, an important early leader in the Church, quoted the prophets of old and said, just as it is written (Acts 15:16-18):

"After these things I will return,
And I shall build the tabernacle of David which has fallen,
And I will rebuild its ruins,
And I will restore it,
So that the rest of mankind may seek the Lord,
And all Gentles that are called by my name,
Says the Lord, who makes these things known from long ago"

James then said, "Brethren listen to me." Do not trouble those who are turning to God from among the gentiles and lay no greater burden on them than these essentials:

That you abstain:
> From things sacrificed to idols
> From blood
> From things strangled
> From fornication

That ended the discussion so the apostles and the Church in Jerusalem all came to agreement, and then they sent Barnabas and Silas with that message to the new churches.

What is going on here? This is a tremendous happening in the new early Church of Jesus Christ. The Kingdom of God (Now the Church) is to include non-Jewish people as this was prophesied from of old. But now instead of the law, given by Moses, mandated for the Jews by God Himself through Moses, we have a new law, the royal law of liberty, as James calls it, in his book of James (2:8-12). The old law is done away with. However, the Church in Jerusalem with the apostles and leaders say there are some essentials which we must lay on you new gentile believers.

Why these particular essentials? One would think they would have at least quoted the Ten Commandments. But no, just four things, which at first seem a little strange. When one examines these four essentials one is struck by the fact that the first three essentials are related to spirit realm matters. Things sacrificed to idols are first a spirit thing. If one is devoted to an idol, one worships the idol and wants the idol to give stuff, prosperity and all that, and promote the idol worshipers welfare. That is why one worships the idol, to get an advantage over others and have good things happen and not have bad things happen.

However, there is another factor in Greek idol worship and probably in other idol worshipping cultures as well, that is, worship of the idol involved fornication with the idol priestesses. Yes, two of the imperatives involve fornication.

Blood, as we moderns understand, carries the oxygen obtained from the air around to each part of the body, to each cell of the body. Air is a symbol of Gods breath as God breathes spirit into each of man to give them life. Prohibiting eating blood indicates one must not eat spirit – one must not absorb spirit, one must respect the spirit, and respect the spirit of an animal, and respect God.

Things strangled are similar. When an animal is strangled, its air is choked off, so again the blood is deprived of air.

Now consider fornication. If three of the four essentials for gentile believers have to do with the spirit realm, surely the other must have to do with the spirit realm also. The Prophet Malachi deals with divorce (Malachi 2:14-16) and says to give heed to your <u>spirit</u>, that you not deal treacherously with the wife of your youth. Thus sexual union in marriage has a spiritual factor! Yes, yes, yes! -- According to that which the Prophet Malachi wrote in the Bible.

So fornication is a spiritual thing! Astounding! This cannot be determined by rational analysis. We would not know this unless the Bible through God's revelation to mankind told us. This fact has very serious ramifications for this race of mankind. Most of modern mankind think sexual corruption is just a fun romp in the hay. They do not know that sexual corruption leads directly to spiritual destruction and death.

Marriage Has a Spiritual Factor

Consider now from the 5th chapter of Ephesians the 25th thru 31st verse:

> "Husbands love your wives, just as also Christ loved the church and gave Himself up for her, so that He might sanctify her, having cleansed her by the washing of water with the word, that he might present to Himself the church in all her glory, having no spot or wrinkle or any such thing; but that she should be holy and blameless. So husbands ought to love their own wives as their own bodies. He who loves his own wife loves himself; for no one hated his own flesh, but nourishes and cherishes it, just as Christ also the church, because we are members of His body.
>
> **'For this reason a man shall leave his father and mother and shall be joined to his wife, and the two shall be one flesh.'**
>
> This mystery is great; but I am speaking with reference to Christ and the Church. Nevertheless, each individual among you also is to love his own wife even as himself and the wife must see that she respects her husband."

Here we have the Apostle Paul explaining the relationship between Christ and His Church. Paul uses as a picture of the Church, the marriage relationship. But Paul goes further and lays out the imperatives in the relationship between male man and female man. This is a great mystery. Paul quotes the Old Testament statement of God that a man and his wife are joined together and are one flesh. Obviously they cannot occupy each other's flesh so becoming one together with each other is a deep spiritual thing where the two intertwine and share soul, spirit, and heart.

Again, this is with the body a four-realm relationship. This is the possessive ideal, but yes, Christians must pursue it in their marriage relationship.

Moab and Balaam

There is an interesting account in the Book of Numbers, Chapters 22 to 25, of a fornication encounter of the Israelites. After they wandered in the wilderness for 40 years and the time came for them to go into the Promised Land, they made their way east of the lands of Moab and Edom to approach the Jordan River valley north of the land of Moab from the east. The sons of Israel were then camped on the plains of Moab on the east side of the Jordan River. Moab was located on a high plateau above the Jordan riff valley. Israel had been forbidden by God to make war on Edom or Moab.

Moab was in great fear of Israel. The King of Moab, Balak, hired the soothsayer, Balaam, son of Beor at Pethor, near the Great River which was most likely the Euphrates. Balak sent for him and offered him huge sums of money to come and curse Israel. It is a great long, interesting story with even an ass talking to Balaam. Balaam was told by God to be very careful and watch what he says for he is not to curse Israel.

Balaam's greed causes him to come, and from the heights of Moab above the valley, is shown the multitude of Israel below on the plain of the Jordan. He tries to curse them. Instead three times he ends up blessing Israel. This makes Balak very angry. He fires Balaam and his Midianite entourage and sends them away.

Before he leaves, Balaam says, "Hey Balak, round up the hot women of Moab and send them down there to play with those Israelites."

So the Moabites invited the Israelites to feasts with sacrifices to Baal, the Moab god, and the people ate and bowed down to their gods and rose up to play. The people joined themselves to Baal of Peor.

Twenty-four thousand Israelites died of plague. Moses was also commanded to slay the transgressors among them with the sword. Then Phinehas son of Eleazar, son of Aaron, Moses brother, observing Cozbi daughter of Zur, a Midianite princess, in the arms of Zimri a prince of the sons of Israel, drove a spear with one thrust through both of them. The plague was checked.

Were the bones of those fornicating Israelites left to bleach in the sun? Were they buried? Were they burned? The text does not say. But those fornicators of Israel were terminated.

Moses then sent 12,000 men, 1,000 from each tribe of Israel, to go to liquidate the Midianites. In the process Balaam and all the women of Midian who had participated in the Balaam trick were killed.

What do we make of this account?   God hates fornication. Understand that fornication is even a fornication against God Himself, as fornication is attaching oneself to the demons as those people of Israel did when attaching themselves to Baal of Peor.

Continuing on from this understanding that fornication leads to an invasion and attachment by demons, let us consider the absorption of evil spirit demons that can destroy the life of man.

Spirits Like a Cup

Our spirits are like a cup, meant to hold God's Spirit. We are given the understanding that the sexual act between a man and a woman in some way provides for union between the male man and the female man - that it has a spiritual dimension. Like their bodies, their spirits and souls and hearts become entwined. Through the sexual act, the male man's spirit becomes part of the female man's spirit, or the cup of the man's spirit receives part of the woman's spirit. The woman's spirit becomes part of the man's spirit, or the cup of the woman's spirit receives part of the man's spirit. The Old Testament Prophet Malachi confirmed the ramification of this spiritual union through the marriage covenant (Malachi 2:15-16).

Understand, here is the essential reason why the law of God so condemns fornication and adultery. As each human person violates these prohibitions, that human person adds to his or her spirit little pieces of each spirit he or she collects along the way. In each one-night stand, each drunken encounter, each affair, and each prostitute, the spirit of each is added to the spirit of the other. Eventually, as sexual encounters multiply, there is very little room for God's Spirit. The guilt becomes so overwhelming and the conscience so calloused, the human finds it very difficult to find and know God and be able then to add God's Spirit to his or her spirit.

In consequence, that human becomes hardened, comes to hate God, and to oppose God in everything he or she can conceive. They are wont to become the enemies of God and extend that into a deep hate of God. They eventually become irrational in their hatred of God and become captives of Satan, that evil being, whose goal is death for as many men and women as possible.

This partially explains the mystery of why advocates of free love and sexual promiscuity seem so adamantly, irrationally opposed to God, whereas other sinners who oppose the law of God, such as thieves and murderers, seldom seem to express violent opposition to God and Jesus, God's goals and programs.

God's Spirit within you can keep evil spirits out of you. The most effective prayer one can ever make is to ask God to prevent all evil spirits from witnessing to you or influencing you. Let your prayer be that only God's Pure and Holy Spirit should witness to you. It works. God answers that prayer! You can no longer be confused as to what to do in difficult choice situations.

As a result of a sexual encounter, a woman's spirit is added to the man's spirit, and a man's spirit is added to a woman's spirit. Can you imagine the consequences of a whore's or gigolo's spirit being added to your spirit? Every evil spirit that ever entered into that whore, performing a sexual act, can now have access to your spirit. Can your bosom take on evil after evil and not be become evil itself? Never! As the Scriptures say, the whore's path leads to death and destruction, and her path leads you down into hell itself.

Can promiscuous sex with college or work friends, or a pick-up at a bar, be any different? You do not know what kind and how many sexual partners he or she may have had. Evil spirits may have been collected from many places and now they have access to you, to your spirit.

Demons, another name for evil spirits, now become manifested in your life as insanities. These demon insanities have access to you, and you can start down the path to insanity yourself. Indeed, fornication is terribly, terribly, destructive.

Paired Monogamous Marriage

Understand that the Apostle Paul's imperative for the Christian believer is that there are only two choices: (1) complete chastity, or (2) one man and one woman in paired monogamous marriage. He received this command from Jesus Himself who quoted the book of Genesis where he said,

> "In the beginning the Creator, God, made them male and female, and said, 'A man shall leave his parents and be joined unto his wife, and they shall become one flesh.' So they are no longer two, but one. Therefore, what God has joined together, let not man separate." (Matthew 19:4-6)

Receive in your understanding the contrast in the spirit realm. Instead of the destruction and death caused by demons living within man, the Christian Scriptures say to the believer:

"Christ Jesus Himself being the cornerstone, in whom the whole building, being fitted together, is growing into a holy temple in the Lord, in whom you also are being built together into a dwelling of God in the Spirit." (Ephesians 2:20-22)

And continuing another quote of spirit power,

"You are not in the flesh but in the Spirit, if indeed the Spirit of God dwells in you. But if anyone does not have the Spirit of Christ, he does not belong to Him. If Christ is in you, though the body is dead because of sin, yet the spirit is alive because of righteousness. But if the Spirit of Him who raised Jesus from the dead dwells in you, He who raised Christ Jesus from the dead will also give life to your mortal bodies through His Spirit who dwells in you." (Romans 8:9-11)

Another statement from Jesus Himself is,

"He who overcomes, I will make him a pillar in the temple of God, and he will not go out from it anymore; and I will write on him the name of God, and the name of the city of God, the new Jerusalem, which comes down out of heaven from God, and My new name. He, who has an ear, let him hear what the Spirit says." (Revelation 3:12-13)

These are marvelous statements of Christian life in the spirit as part of the temple of God the Almighty.

In the Christian life we must walk according to God's Spirit. For with the Spirit of the life of Jesus Christ we are free from the condemnation of sin and death. God sent His Son, the only begotten of God, of the same substance as God, to be condemned as sin in the body of His flesh, so that we who walk according to God's Spirit, are no longer slaves to sin. We are free from the penalty of sin, but we are not sinless. We have received life eternal.

To sum up, the Spirit of Him who raised Jesus from the dead, dwelling and living within your spirit, gives eternal life to your mortal body.

In following chapters the contrary to living in the spirit is presented. Examples of cultures that know not God are given, and then the mechanism that God seemingly uses to rule in His creation is discussed. An example of false teaching is presented. Then this writing will return to the imperative of paired monogamous marriage.

EIGHT

Wrath of God on American Cultures

From the Book of Romans Chapter 1 starting with the 18th verse:

"For the wrath of God is revealed from heaven against all ungodliness and unrighteousness of men who suppress the truth in unrighteousness, because that which is known about God is evident within them; for God made it evident to them. For since the creation of the world His invisible attributes, His eternal power and divine nature, have been clearly seen, being understood through what has been made, so that they are without excuse. For even though they knew God they did not honor Him as God or give thanks, but they became futile in their speculations, and their foolish heart was darkened. Professing to be wise, they became fools, and exchanged the glory of the incorruptible God for an image in the form of corruptible man and of birds and four-footed animals and crawling creatures.

"Therefore God gave them over to the lusts of their hearts to impurity, so that their bodies would be dishonored among them. For they exchanged the truth of God for a lie, and worshiped and served the creature rather than the Creator, who is blessed forever, Amen.

"For this reason God gave them over to degrading passions; for their women exchanged the natural function for that which is unnatural, and in the same way also the men abandoned the natural function of the women and burned in their desire toward one another, men with men committing indecent acts and receiving in their own person the due penalty of their error.

"And just as they did not see fit to acknowledge God any longer, God gave them over to a depraved mind, to do the things that are not proper, being filled with all unrighteousness, wickedness, greed, evil, full of envy, murder, strife, deceit, malice, gossips, slanderers, haters of God, insolent, arrogant, boastful, inventors of evil, disobedient to parents, without understanding, untrustworthy, unloving, unmerciful; and although they know the ordinance of God, that those who practice such things are worthy of death, they not only do the same, but give hearty approval to those who practice them."

What an indictment of our modern age - women abandoning the natural sexual function of women and men abandoning women and lusting for one another. The homosexual agenda is now being accepted as normal by a majority of Americans. Paul clearly lays out the consequences. A due penalty for this error is to be received throughout the culture. Ultimately all kinds of evil permeate the society, and then insanity follows. Depraved minds start to rule the country. It is here in America now. This is the wrath of God. This is God's wrath on man when the truth of God is suppressed and abandoned.

Historical Example of North America

Let me present historical examples of cultures which knew not God.

The Conquistadors from Spain sent several armies into the New World of America in search of gold, silver, jewels, slaves, and productive lands that could be worked for profit.[4] In 1521 Cortez and his very small army group conquered Mexico and in 1532 Hernando Pizarro and his tiny army group conquered the Incas in South America and found plenty gold.[5] Others conquered in Central America.

Three expeditions went into North America. The first in 1528 led by Pamfilo de Narvaez with about 400 Spanish fighting men landed near Tampa Bay in modern Florida and was a complete disaster with only four survivors, one of which was Cabeza de Vaca, who had become a slave to the indigenous natives, suffered lots of abuse, and after eight years managed to get to Mexico with three companions.

The second in 1539 was led by Hernando De Soto with about 600 Spaniards with lots of horses, pigs, and dogs.[6] They wandered around Florida, Alabama, Georgia, Tennessee, the Carolinas, Arkansas, and up and down the Mississippi, and eventually after a few years left.

About half survived and made it to Mexico. The third expedition was led by Francisco Coronado in 1541 in which an army of about 400 Spaniards plus native auxiliaries marched from Mexico up the West coast of Mexico along the Sea of Cortez into Arizona, California, New Mexico, and Texas and got up as far as Kansas and Nebraska, found no gold, and then returned to Mexico.

Chroniclers and others with the armies wrote down their experiences and observations concerning these expeditions and recorded them for posterity. The various tribes of people encountered by these conquistadors and their culture and practice are described by these writers.

Hundreds of different tribes all speaking different languages and having sundry different cultures were encountered. Some of these peoples were cannibals and ate each other. Most made war on each other. Some were established highly organized civilizations with extensive rituals and cultural forms. Some lived by agriculture, some by hunting and fishing, and some by gathering various fruits, insects, and anything one could eat. By studying these accounts carefully one can come to understand a little of the nature and conflict of cultures, those which function well and survive and those which do not work well and not survive against their enemies.

Many of these cultures practiced sodomy and berdache activity, especially those in the region of modern coastal Texas north to the central plains of the United States. Those who practiced such corrupt activity did not survive. They are gone and forgotten. The ones who practiced agriculture, and in which no homosexual type activity was recorded as practiced, such as the Zuni, survive to this day. Is there a lesson in this? Yes, homosexual practice is terribly destructive to a society and to a culture. Those cultures which practice such deteriorate and do not survive.

Spanish expeditions in the 1700's into Texas recorded the same effect.[7] One hundred forty different tribes were observed and recorded during the period of 1689 to 1768. Several cultures in Texas still practiced such sexual corruption into the 1700's, but as one chronicler noted, these tribes were wiped out by their Spanish friends and their Comanche enemies.

It has been shown in this writing that human sexual encounters have a spiritual factor. Deviate sexual practice is terribly destructive. Why is that? Is such practice just contrary to God's law, or is there a deep spiritual dimension to the thing that destroys human kind? Apparently so. That is why such activity is contrary to the fundamental nature of God. God made man to enjoy fellowship with man. Human sexual corruption destroys that fellowship with God.

God has given man a taste of intimate potential fellowship with God by the example of the sexual union experience with one's one and only spouse. God has given to man this exotic ecstatic experience, and established the pattern so as to demonstrate to man his ultimate devotion is only to be to God, the One who has made him and loves him.

One anthropological researcher has maintained that Neanderthals had a societal behavior like that observed in herds of elk and troops of baboons where the herd or troop of females is serviced by one alpha male. In such herd type tribal structure the herd alpha male has to constantly fight off challenges by other males to maintain his dominance and keep possession of his herd or harem. In baboon troops the young males without any females around practice sodomy. This was probably true of Neanderthals. Some researchers claim that the human race has genetic material in their genes from Neanderthals and other humanoid animal species. The assumption must then be made that somewhere in the past some humans engaged in bestial activity wherein such genetic contributions to the human race were made.

If, in fact, a few of the man race in the past engaged in such severely corrupt activity, one can understand the internal drive within some of those corrupt of man to participate in and continue the ugly awful practice. This was caused by the corruption introduced and made a psychological drive within man by the genetic material contributed from these animal humanoid species to the human race.

Now, of course, a lot of this is pure conjecture but one can perceive the understanding of the corruption contributed to the human race by bestiality and sodomy. The human race must still be driven by this genetic influence even today as evidenced by the modern homosexual political movement in which homosexual deviant intellectuals advocate such deviant corrupting behavior. That is why God so strongly prohibits human sexual contact with beasts and other homosexual activity. It leads to death and destruction.

Understand that Satan, that fallen angel who hates God, desires death for all mankind. He hates God and all that God stands for. Therefore, Satan, whom God permits to operate in the spiritual realm, seeks the destruction of all mankind. What better way is there for Satan to destroy mankind than through easy sexual misconduct?

Historical Example of Mexico

The account of the Spanish conquistador Cortez, who with a handful of soldiers conquered Mexico, is quite astounding.[5]

How could maybe an initial 600 Spaniards conquer about twenty million people? This huge astounding population estimate made by the Spanish chroniclers is about the same population that occupies the Mexican mountain basin today. Many modern writers discount this estimate and say it is too large. But the chroniclers are believed in most everything else they report, and so why should this report of twenty million people not be believed?

The tribes that occupied the large central Mexican hanging basin practiced human sacrifice. The Spanish chroniclers estimated 100,000 (that is one hundred thousand!) people a year were sacrificed to their pagan gods! What a stench in God's nostrils! Can you not believe that God would permit Satan to so stir up the Spaniards and give them such a lust for gold so as to go to Mexico and conquer, and eventually depopulate the place?

Yes, those Aztecs and other neighboring tribes were destroyed and a remnant was incorporated into a new Spanish/indigenous race which flourishes yet today. One of the most amazing things of the whole enterprise was that the Spaniards did it in the name of God. They forced conversion of the tribes to the religion of Roman Catholic Christianity. The choice was to convert or be a slave. Most slaves died as the diseases the Spaniards brought with them from Europe wiped the indigenous people out, especially the slaves. Human sacrifice in Mexico was terminated. Homosexual practice in Texas and the American plains was terminated. The Spaniards gave them no quarter.

During the course of Hernando De Soto's wanderings in the southeast and central United States, his army had a battle with Native Americans in which the chroniclers say 5,000 warriors were killed. His army then crossed the Mississippi River and proceeded into present day Arkansas and some of Hernando's people even went west out into the plains and reported seeing buffalo. Finding no easy gold and suffering some nasty vicissitudes, Hernando got sick and died.

The decision was then made to evacuate and survive and try to make a journey to Mexico. The army then built a number of substantial boats. They abandoned the 1,000 or more sundry tribal slaves they have captured and incorporated into their expedition to the tender mercies of the other warlike indigenous tribes. They then loaded what they could into the boats and descended the Mississippi. Going down the river they encountered large numbers of warriors wherein several more battles were fought. Eventually about 300 Spaniards survived and made it to Mexico.

De Soto messed with a very large number of indigenous people. They had an extensive agricultural civilization with large amounts of stored maize which the army of the Spaniards stole and lived on in their wanderings. The Spaniards traveled about with a number of horses, lots of pigs, and numerous dogs. They fed tribal owned maize to the horses, the pigs lived on acorns and other nuts found in the forest, and the

Spaniards fed human slaves to their dogs as anybody not obedient to the conquistadors was fed to the dogs when the dogs got hungry.

These indigenous people built high mounds of dirt, the mounds like those of Mexico. A little thinking about all this and why they built mounds in their cities leads one to the observation that these mounds, too, like those of the Aztecs in Mexico were probably used for human sacrifice. Why a mound? If one wants to keep a population under control, especially those captured from enemies, they are intimidated, put to work to keep them occupied, kept full of fear so they obey and not run away. What better method than to sacrifice some of them with an elaborate ceremony that could be viewed by many, many people just watching the happenings on top of the mound, all from a distance?

The Aztecs even had a shaped rounded rock so the priest who was doing the killing had an easy time of it when the knife was plunged into the breast of the sacrifice to remove the victim's heart so it could be lifted up for all to see. When Cortez' army retreated from Mexico City, from a distance they watched their captured friends and fellow solders die the death of being sacrificed to a pagan god. No wonder when Cortez army returned, they obliterated the place.

So come the Spaniards of De Soto to the Mississippi valley, the central part of the present United States and they leave the place wasted. They eat up the maize and let their horses and pigs destroy the grain fields. They spread the European diseases of humans, horses, pigs, and dogs all over the place. They leave devastation in their wake, but an end is put to human sacrifice.

About 134 years later the French expedition of Louis Jolliet and Jacques Marquette descended the Mississippi River on a voyage of discovery. They reported the Mississippi valley to be essentially uninhabited. How is that possible? An extensive civilization reduced to nothing? Now today that same land is a bread basket. That land feeds the world! That same land was uninhabited? Yes. The stench of human sacrifice and homosexual practice reached God's nostrils. Enough is enough. De Soto's army did their thing.

What is to be learned from all this? I cannot and do not speak for God. God's ways are unfathomable. His ways are past even knowing. We can only observe and learn a lesson. God has said He hates perversion and human sacrifice and murder. We know that. Yet about sixty million little human beings have been sacrificed to the fire god of the abortion clinic incinerators and dumpster landfills in the United States. Has the stench of this yet reached God's nostrils? Yes, indeed!

Historical Example of the Pacific Northwest

During the period from about 1785 to 1798 several explorers from different countries investigated the Pacific Northwest of the American continent. In 1792, Robert Gray, a private person and a businessman of the United States from Boston, in his ship, Columbia, sailed across the sandbar at the mouth of the Columbia River and gave the name of his ship to that magnificent river of the west.[8]

At about the same time Captain Vancouver of the British Navy was exploring the northwest coast of America and encountered Gray. They discussed the possible existence and location of the great river of the west. Vancouver did not think it was where Gray indicated it might be located so went on to explore the Straights of Juan de Fuca, Vancouver Island, and Puget Sound.

They reported that the indigenous people of Nootka Sound where they took their ships for succor were cannibals. They ate the flesh of their enemies and frequently ate their slaves. Slaves were captured in their frequent warfare. They also had human sacrifice. Polygamy was practiced and one had as many wives as one could buy.

At Chickleset Sound, Chief Cassacan of Nitinat was discovered to have venereal disease. The chief said he had sold a slave girl to the British, and when they left they gave the slave girl back, and then she died. She gave the disease to the chief and he gave it to his wife. His wife was now near death and the chief was not long for this world. Cassacan's tribe also got the small pox from a recent visit by a Spanish ship in the Straights of Juan de Fuca.

North of Vancouver Island on the present British Columbia coast were the lands of the Haida, Tlingit, Bella Coola, and the Tsimshian. They enslaved their captives and made human sacrifices of them.

The great British Naval explorer, James Cook, reported that he found venereal disease in Maui in the Hawaiian Islands when he returned there from a northern exploration to the Bering Strait. His ship had visited the island of Kauai the previous year. Cook was afraid of that evil disease spreading, but it spread from his ships despite his efforts. But consider that Maui is a two island hop from Kauai and a considerable distance across a lot of ocean. The disease from Cook's ship had spread that far in less than a year. It was not long after this that King Kamehameha from the Big Island conquered the whole of the islands.

All of these accounts indicate vast widespread moral corruption among the indigenous people of North America and even among the people of the Hawaiian Islands. Those peoples did not survive. European man's diseases and moral corruption terminated them.

Historical Example of California

One of the great mysteries of early exploration of North America is California. The first attempt at seeing what the west coast of North America looked like was done by Juan Cabrillo. He discovered what is now called the port of San Diego Bay in 1542, located at about 33 degrees north latitude.

He then sailed along the coast north to present day Santa Barbara at about 35 degrees north latitude. He reported large numbers of indigenous people between San Diego and Santa Barbara. These people apparently lived on fish, seaweed, and shellfish from the ocean and acorns from the oak trees that grew in abundance.

An attempt to sail further north was thwarted by storms and high winds. His ship probably sailed as far north as the mouth of the Klamath River in California at about 42 degrees north. Almost never did his ship see land as they attempted to do this too early in the year when storms still happen off the coast of California and they were afraid of the very rocky seacoast. The marvelous port of modern San Francisco was not discovered.

In a fight with some indigenous people back near San Barbara, Juan received a leg injury which probably got infected and this eventually killed him. The second in command tried to continue with additional exploration as he was instructed to do, but gave it up and returned to Mexico.

Sir Francis Drake from England made an expedition in 1580 into the Pacific Ocean by going around the continent of South America to the South.[9] He got lost in a storm after transitioning the Straits of Magellan and was blown south of the continent thus giving his name to the strait between South America and Antarctica. Drake then turned back north along the west coast of South America. He then plundered the Spanish ships and towns on the coasts of South and Central America and took on so much gold and silver he had to replace the ballast in his ship with the gold and silver.

Drake was a marvelous seaman who figured out the nature of the global winds. To get to North America he sailed far out into the Pacific going northwest with the easterly trade winds between 30 degrees south latitude and 30 degrees north latitude. He then turned northeast to intersect the northwesterly winds in the Pacific at latitudes north of 30 degrees north. At 50 degrees north he sailed east to land on Vancouver Island in present day Canada.

He explored the north coast of North America along the Canadian coast probably to as far north as 60 degrees latitude and then decided there was most likely not a so called Straight of Anion north of the American continent for him to use to get back to England by such a northeasterly route.

He then sailed south, most likely between Vancouver Island and the mainland of Canada, where he reported a marvelous place to establish an English civilization, most probably on the east coast of Vancouver Island north of present day Victoria, British Columbia. This area was very well populated with people. Drake named it New Albion.

Sailing down to about 43 degrees he found a small bay on the coast of Oregon where he could clean his ships and not be bothered by too many people. He had captured a smaller Spanish ship and had it cleaned too. Drake then departed for the Orient across the Pacific Ocean and eventually reached England with his vast load of gold making Queen Elizabeth of England and himself rich with stolen Spanish gold.

The second smaller ship that Drake apparently left behind in Oregon was never heard from again. Drake left instructions that it was to sail north and again look for the mythical Straits of Anion. Since we now know that strait does not exist, the ship captain most likely eventually sailed his small ship back to New Albion, as Drake called it, or to Oregon, or even into California.

Records of where Drake sailed in North America became an English State secret. The chroniclers have tried to decipher the assorted information Drake tried to communicate to some of his friends and others, but his queen, Elizabeth of England, in her paranoia of the Spaniards, forbid publication of Drakes reports in hopes of secrecy, as Spanish spies were everywhere in England. Remember this was just a few years before the great Spanish Armada attack on England.

Information has indicated vast cannibalism, war, murder, and sexual corruption among the large number of indigenous people in North America.

There is a very intriguing account based on circumstantial evidence that that crew of that second Drake ship made it to California. Drake left instructions they were to wait at least three years for him to return. Drake tried to get ships back to California from England, but the Spanish thwarted the attempt every time. A man by the name of Morena, who may have been a navigator Drake captured from the Spanish and forced to accompany him, who may also have been the Captain of the Bark left behind in Oregon. He seems to have journeyed down to Mexico about four years after Drake's departure.

The Spanish, following their normal mode of cruelty, probably put him in prison and most likely tortured him to make him tell all he knew. He seemed to have quite misled the Spaniards as the Spaniards created the Straits of Juan de Fuca between Vancouver Island and the north coast of the present state of Washington without leaving any record of any Spanish ship or sailor ever going to the Straits of Juan de Fuca to find it, or prove it did not provide a way to the Atlantic.

Early Spanish maps showed a Straits of Juan de Fuca. They assumed it was the beginning of the Straits of Anion connecting the Pacific Ocean with the Atlantic. They must have got that misleading information from Morena.

For 200 years after Drake and Morena, Spanish maps showed California to be an island, even though the expedition of Coronado clearly established that the Sea of Cortez ended at the mouth of the Colorado River, making California part of the mainland and not an Island.

For many years the Spanish sent a ship and sometimes a fleet of ships yearly to the Philippines from Mexico across the Pacific for a very lucrative trade. These ships sailed with the easterly trade winds to the Philippines, and on the return trip to Mexico, they would sail north to pick up the westerly winds at 40 degrees north and sail east to about Cape Mendocino on the California Coast which is at a little less than 40½ degrees north and then follow the coast south to Mexico. In all of about 200 years they did not discover the marvelous port of San

Francisco Bay, even though scurvy took a terrible toll on Spanish sailors from the long voyage. They badly needed a place to rest, succor, and recuperate on the coast of California but never found one. There is even a report of one ghost ship from the orient with no sailors left alive, drifting off the coast of Mexico. That is how badly they suffered from scurvy.

It seems the prisoner of the Spaniards, Morena, misled them, probably to protect his fellow shipmates left behind somewhere in Washington, Oregon or California from Spanish cruelty. The Spaniards most likely would have butchered them like they butchered the French Huguenots.

When the Spaniards finally did discover San Francisco Bay in 1769, it was quite by accident during a land expedition from Mexico up through Baja California to the north as Gaspar de Portola got lost trying to find Monterrey Bay and stumbled onto San Francisco Bay.

A diary report by the Spaniard, Fr. Juan Crespi, who also had been with Portola, made a reconnaissance led by Captain Don Pedro Fages with about twelve soldiers and some muleteers along the east side of San Francisco Bay to the Carquinez Strait. They climbed Mt. Diablo and got a good look at the Sacramento and San Joaquin valleys, the first Europeans to do so (Diary of Juan Crespi, Online Books).

Crespi wrote they encountered very light skinned natives on Strawberry Creek, now on the campus of the University of California in Berkeley, and more light skinned people near the present city of Danville east of Berkeley on their way back to Monterey. They had traveled from Berkeley up to the Carquinez Strait where they discovered the main arm of San Francisco Bay, the Sacramento River, and decided they could not cross it.

They reached the Carquinez Strait on March 30, 1772. Natives from the other side of the strait rowed their boats across to meet with them. They were very light skinned, some with red hair, with beards, and very good looking. To a Spaniard somebody who looks like a

Spaniard or Englishmen must be much better looking than an aborigine. It is interesting that even though Captain Fages wanted very much to explore around to Bodega Bay in the northwest from there, he gave up here and decided to return to Monterey.

Carquinez Strait is very intimidating to a pilot of a small boat. I have been there and had a very close call of my own when I crossed the Sacramento River late one evening about 10 miles or so to the east of the main narrow of the strait. In my life I have been a risk taker and I had experience in operating very small boats on the ocean. A friend and I went fishing and we had to cross the Sacramento River to get back to the dock where we had rented the boat on the north side of the Strait.

We were in a very bad situation with high wind. The outboard motor propeller was coming out of the water with the up and down of each wave so I had to throttle back and yet still have enough power to keep the bow into the wind. If the boat turned we would be swamped by the waves. We probably had life jackets, but with those waves, we would have not survived. My companion did exactly what I said for him to do to keep the boat bow to the wind and the oncoming huge waves; otherwise we would have swamped and not made it. At the top of the wave I had to hang on to the motor to keep from falling down to him in the bow, and at the bottom of the wave he was way above me and he had to hang on laying in the bottom of the bow, or he would have fallen down on me. It was a real challenge. That college friend never went anywhere with me again.

There are almost always strong winds in the Carquinez Strait as it is located in the gap in the coastal mountain range of California where the wind always blows one way or the other. I can understand why Captain Fages did not want to cross. The fact that the local natives were not at all intimidated to cross the straight in their little craft to meet with him indicates to me they had some heritage of sea faring. Were these descendants of Drakes men? Who knows?

Another possibility for the light skin and beards of the natives is from the crew of one of the Cavendish ships, another English buccaneer, who after plundering the Spanish Ship, Santa Ana, off Cabo San Lucas in Baja California in 1587, probably sailed north. The ship, Contents, of 60 tons was never heard from again. This raid on Spanish shipping was seven years after Drake did his thing. They most likely knew Drake had left a ship with English sailors on the northwest coast so they went to look for it and Drakes land of New Albion, or perhaps have another look for the Straits of Anion.

The most remarkable thing is the Spaniards ignored California for almost 200 years. There are probably good reasons for this. Because of sea temperatures with warm current offshore and cold current near the shore, there are almost always fogs of one kind or another as one approaches the North American continent. Winter and early spring are probably the best time to have good visibility to explore the seacoast but that is also the time of the possibility of severe, dangerous, Pacific storms.

Another factor is political. The Spaniards were ruled by a king with an autocratic bureaucracy, severely destroying individual initiative, and usually immensely delaying things. One viceroy of Mexico even ordered everybody not to explore the west coast of North America because he did not want any information about it to be given to the English. So not discovering anything meant the English would never learn anything. Maybe his fears were correct as both Drake and Cavendish made great hauls plundering the Spanish.

None of these possible reasons fully explain why this most marvelous land of California lay undiscovered by Europeans for 200 years.

Another very remarkable thing is that when the Spaniards finally did come, the indigenous people of California who were very numerous, were very poor and had an extremely low level of civilization. The people lived on seeds, acorns, fish, seaweed, and shellfish. Yet California is an extremely bountiful place. Early exploration into the central valley revealed extensive herds of elk, antelope, and deer. Also there were huge, very dangerous grizzly bears. It is, and was, a very beautiful, bountiful place.   Again there are reports of homosexual activity and sexual corruption among the indigenous people.   Is that corrupt practice the cause of such poverty and low level of civilization?

There is an account by Fray Antonio de la Ascension who was with the Vizcaino expedition to Upper California in 1602 who described the land around present day Long Beach and Los Angeles to be very well populated, the land being very rich. A petty king of sorts paddled his large boat out to Vizcaino's ship and invited him to come to the land, and he would provide them with food, and with all they needed. The king saw that the Spaniards had no women on their ship with them, took pity on them, and offered to each Spaniard ten fine women each. Vizcaino declined the deal.   The Spaniards saw lots of fires, lots of smoke, and lots of people.

When they got to the region of Monterey, Fray Ascension reported many fires, people, elk, and whales, with fierce bears feeding on dead whales washed ashore.   Then the Spaniards ignored the place for 170 years.

The almost legendary attorney, Edmund Randolph, winner of a huge lawsuit for the United States over a mercury mine in California, and an enemy of the vigilance committees in San Francisco, wrote a history of California.[10] Randolph received some of his information from the records of Friar Francisco Palou, a contemporary of Fr. Juniper Sierra.   This was published by the University of California in 1926. Randolph's history, of course, is second hand information. He also had access to other original documents of early explorers.   He was an important personage in creating and developing the state of California from 1850 to 1860.

Randolph wrote of the indigenous cultures of California. Quoting briefly, he described California aborigines as despicable types of mankind, living in petty groups. "The bear more lord than he." "No human tenant occupied the most delightful of habitation." The people lived on mussels, acorns, blackberries, strawberries, fish, whale blubber when the whale stranded, and wore no clothes. Marriage and divorce were quick and easy. If they quarreled, the individual simply said, "I have thrown him away", or "I have thrown her away". If a man married a woman, he also married all her sisters. Polygamy and incest was widespread.

The Spanish initiated a mission process to Christianize those indigenous people. The Spanish in their autocratic way were successful in extending the mission system north into Upper California, baptizing many into the Roman Catholic Faith. The mission system created vast self-supporting agricultural and stock raising communities of indigenous people ruled over by priests and soldiers. People who resisted the system usually left and migrated to the central valley where they eventually became known as the Horse Thief Indians because they were fond of horse meat. Disease introduced by Europeans, including small pox, measles, and venereal, took their toll on the indigenous people. The mission system continued in Upper California from about 1769 when San Francisco Bay was discovered, to about 1823 when Mexico took over as Mexico then became independent from Spain.

Under the Mexicans, with the secularization of the missions in the 1830's, the indigenous people of California continued to disappear rather rapidly. The secularization left the Indians largely homeless as the mission lands were deeded to ranchers. Most of the indigenous survivors wandered away to join the so called Horse Thief Tribe. Punitive expeditions of soldiers and settlers also reduced the Horse Thief Indian population. After gold was discovered, the wave of American 49ers rather brutally, quickly, finished the job, and the indigenous people of California almost disappeared.

In turn the rancher civilization of Californios, as the California Mexicans were called, was quickly assimilated into the 49er miner wave of immigration, and subsequent huge waves of immigration of United States residents into California. One Mexican landowner, Luis Peralta who owned most of the land where today the cities of Oakland, Alameda, and Berkeley are, said to his sons when gold was discovered:

"My sons, God has given this gold to the Americans, had He desired us to have it, He would have given it to us ere now. Therefore, go not after it, but let others go. Plant your lands, and reap; these be your best gold-fields, for all must eat while they live."

Subsequently, in complete disregard of the ownership rights of the Peralta family, squatters moved in on Peralta land and laid out the City of Oakland.[11]   Litigation followed where everybody loses but the attorneys. The attorneys had a very profitable field day in the early American occupation of California.

NINE

God's Rule, Non-linear Systems

How does God rule in His creation? As a start to this difficult-to-understand question, consider the consequential operations of non-linear systems.

Temperature of the earth

A good example of a non-linear system is the temperature of the earth.

The surface temperature of the earth is influenced by the following factors and perhaps many others:

Direct radiation intensity onto the earth from the sun
Radiation intensity from the earth out into space
Cloud cover or dust in the air that reflects the radiation energy
    of the sun back out into space
Chemicals or gases in the atmosphere of the earth which trap
    the radiation energy escaping from the earth
Nuclear reactions within the earth which generate heat
Conductivity path of the heat within the earth to the surface
Convection paths of the heat from within the molten earth

From an engineering standpoint, given all these methods of heating and cooling of the earth, the temperature of the earth is a result of a complex non-linear system.

That conclusion has several very serious ramifications. Most of us are familiar with linear systems. A linear system is like the foot feed on your automobile. The harder you press on the foot feed the faster your automobile travels. Most of us think in terms of linear systems.

Related to this is the principle of causality. The principle of causality says some things have a cause. For example, the harder you push on your foot feed, the faster the automobile goes. Pushing on the foot feed is the cause of the faster automobile.

When something happens, most people think in terms of what caused that something to happen. Things which have a direct cause are closely related to linear systems. Most of all the marvelous things and inventions of mankind which we moderns happily use and in which we rejoice were developed through the principal of causality. Electronics is a great marvelous example of linear systems and the principal of casualty. Electronic systems are linear systems. Your printer, computer, and telephone work and do what they are supposed to do because they were developed using causality and linear system analysis.

Many people try to force linear causality thinking onto most other phenomena. For example, cholesterol in human bodies is related to blockage of arteries in the human blood stream so some try to lower the cholesterol in the bloodstream as a way of reducing strokes and heart attacks. It is not that simple. Lowering heart attacks and strokes is a very complicated non-linear system. Lowering the cholesterol in the blood stream may or may not have the desired effect on the lowering the frequency of strokes and heart attacks.

The Food and Drug Administration (FDA) of the United States has the responsibility of approving or disapproving the sales of drugs which are supposed to lower the cholesterol in the blood stream and, therefore, lower the risk of heart attacks and strokes. To get a drug approved for sale, the FDA demands a double blind statistical study to show the statistical effectiveness of the drug. This is a good example of a non-linear system and how to analyze and handle non-linear systems.

In order for a statistical study to show effectiveness of a drug to be approved for sale by the FDA, usually at least 3,000 data points must be provided. The FDA would rather have 30,000 data points to have a higher confidence level. Obtaining data points is very expensive; so therefore, the FDA will sometimes let something get approved with not less than about 3,000 data points.

As a very simple example of a non-linear system, consider the rolling of a pair of dice. The result of a rolling of a pair of dice is a number between two and twelve. Since rolling of a pair of dice has been observed many, many times, a statistical distribution of the result has been produced. This results is a probability of a certain outcome. For example, the probability of a two coming up from a roll is one in thirty-six. That is, if one continues to roll the dice again and again, on the average the chance of obtaining a two is one time in every thirty-six rolls of the dice. This is a very simple non-linear system. Every other number showing up on the dice has its own probability. When one rolls the dice one cannot know the result of what the next roll will be. One can only know the probability of what might show up.

So is the temperature of the earth. The temperature of the earth tomorrow or next year or the next century cannot be predicted, but only the distribution of the set of resulting possible temperatures. In order to know the potential distribution, many data points have to be observed. In order to have a real good idea of what the outcome will be for next year, using the type of the analysis for non-linear systems used by the FDA, one should have 30,000 years of data, which, of course, we do not have.

Even then, perhaps during the next 30,000 years of observation, some important event influencing the temperature of the earth may not yet have ever happened. For example, volcano discharge of dirt, rock, and gas into the atmosphere has an effect on the earth temperature. The distribution and frequency of volcano happenings has never really been well charted. Yet a year was recorded sometime in the 1600's when there was a year with no summer and crops did not grow in North America. Some analysts have attributed it to a volcano happening.

Even more disastrous events are meteorite happenings. My ole quantum mechanics professor at Cal was a very interesting, very talented person. He used to own a bright red, hot, sports car - unusual for a physics professor at that time. Louis Alverez was on the airplane that followed the one that dropped the first atomic bomb on Japan. His purpose was to measure the amount and force of the blast. He was a brave man as the potential size of the blast could only be estimated beforehand.

After he taught me and many others lots of wonderful quantum mechanics, Louis became a key person in developing the Bubble Chamber for observing and measuring paths of nuclear particles. For that he received the Nobel Prize in Physics.

When Louis got old, he retired and wandered about the earth with his son who was an archeologist. As a result of digging in lots of places, Louis observed the strata of the deposits where his son was trying to determine the age of something. He observed very interesting stuff in the rock layers from several different widespread places on the earth showing a pattern. Meteorites come from space with certain amount of trace elements in their content not normally observed in quantity in the crust of the earth. Louis saw a pattern repeated which he measured by isotope density. He made suggestions to his son, and they came up with the nemesis theory of the sun.

The sun orbits with another star and this star and the sun come close to each other, perhaps their solar systems even pass through each other, about every 26 million years. When that happens the earth get hits by many meteorites, some perhaps being very large, thus having very devastating consequences for the earth. This theory substantiates the observation that 70 million years or so ago, a large meteorite hit the Yucatan peninsula in Mexico. That event destroyed much life on earth and was responsible for the termination of the dinosaurs.

All of these happenings are non-linear and cannot be predicted. Statistical distributions are the only thing that can be used to estimate what might happen down the road in the future, especially as to the temperature of the earth.

Therefore, the temperature of the earth cannot be predicted.

Simulations: Devices and Military Operations

Consider another example of non-linear systems analysis. In the course of my life I began gainful employment as an Electronic Engineer doing research and developing microwave devices as an employee for a contractor in the defense industry of the United States. You might consider me to have been a cold war warrior. I began to build computer models of microwave devices called Cross Field Amplifiers in order to design and build those devices. I was one of the first to write computer programs to model physical systems. I started doing this in the late 1950s.

A few years later I had my own business and was a subcontractor involved in the design and creation of computer models which were to be an aid in determining the design of the force level requirements of the military forces of the United States. A huge computer program, which eventually evolved into a type of computer language, was written which modeled battlefield scenarios to determine what force levels would be needed in the event of any type of war.

Once a battlefield scenario was created, the computer program would be used to estimate the outcome of a possible battle. This computer program eventually was used to analyze and compute the results with combinations of ground forces, naval forces, and air forces.

At one time I was assigned the task of determining the number of F4 equivalents required to obtain a 0.95 confidence level to win any possible war on the Korean Peninsula. The F4 was a warplane in the US inventory which had suburb air to ground firepower capability. Its firepower could be used as a measurement of an equivalent capability of any other airplane in the inventory, compared with any other airplane, including those of the Chicom's (military slang for Chinese Communists). Each airplane type would have its F4 equivalent in firepower as a percentage of the F4 capability.

This was a very interesting task. A Korean War scenario is interesting because in the past there had been was a war on the Korean Peninsula which involved vertical envelopments, naval envelopments, and a lot of air to ground ordinance, so allowing insight and comparisons to be made. A complex scenario was constructed which would, in a computer model sort of way, represent the war.

Once the computer scenario was created it could be exercised to determine the outcome of a possible war. The really marvelous thing about the computer creation, was one could exercise it again and again over and over to determine multiple outcomes by varying different input parameters in the scenario. In fact, computers are so fast one could calculate the result millions of times.

To solve the assigned problem, the many entry parameters were randomized using a random number generator. The scenario had many input parameters, such as Chicom distribution of forces, effectiveness of the F4, choice of where the navel envelopment would be put ashore, and what not else. It was a very complicated scenario. Using random number generators, the scenario was exercised millions of times. One could then determine a statistical distribution of the results of all these scenario exercises.

From the distribution and varying the number of F4 equivalent airplanes in the scenarios, the number of F4 equivalent airplanes to win the war to a 0.95 confidence level was determined. It turned out one had to use the total industrial capability of the USA for decades making F4s to achieve that result.

That was probably good news to the war planners, as most military men want as much force and firepower as possible. The constraint is how much money they can convince the Congress of the United States to give them.

This is a good example of a non-linear system. A Korean type war has many, many input factors. An actual war is extremely complex and the resulting outcome of an actual war cannot be determined before the war. However, one can create a distribution of possible model outcomes and then make a probability estimate of what might happen to determine the estimated force level to be needed to be successful.

This is how non-linear systems must be analyzed. One cannot predict the future temperature of the surface of the earth. Only God knows the future temperature of the earth. Man can make estimates of the probability distribution of future temperature based on a distribution obtained from a large number of measurements in the past. But then the result is only based on the results of past measurements. This does not include any new thing that might be introduced into a potential scenario.

For example, the Chicoms might come up with a new way to fight that would destroy the usefulness of the Korean model scenario. Similarly, a large meteorite hitting the earth putting huge amounts of dust into the air, or a huge volcano discharge with lots of gas and dust, would negate all the estimates of earth temperature based on the recorded past.

In another interesting study I was to investigate the tradeoff of how to use the military force of fast attack submarines of the USA Navy. Nuclear fast attack submarines so far have never been used in actual warfare. The question was asked, "Should the submarines be used in constructing a submarine barrier line from Norway to north of the British Iles, to Iceland, to Greenland, to intercept and interdict Soviet submarines from the Arctic Ocean as they try to transit the barrier, or should the submarines be used to protect convoys of merchant shipping to support land forces in Europe from a massive Soviet tank invasion." Again, this is another very interesting non-linear problem with huge potential payoff.

The Navy spent a lot of its time and money trying to determine the probability of a kill on a Soviet submarine trying to transit the barrier. But if the US fast attack submarines were best used to protect ship logistic convoys in order to win the war, the Navy was wasting its money. Non-linear problems can only be investigated by the use of statistical analysis.

Does God Hate Evil?

Mentally reflecting on the stated examples of non-linear understanding, let us examine the principle of this writing that God hates evil and how God seems to handle evil. Understand, as was said before, I make no claim or have any basis in my thinking in prophesy or predicting. God rules supremely; God is very patient, and waits and waits for men to repent and change their evil ways. Nevertheless, God's law, and God's ruling principles remain true, and ultimately, are alone enforced by God.

God is in the statistics of happenings. The Bible says God determines the outcome of each roll of the dice. Every little event is controlled and determined by God in His omnipotent power. God made the universe and everything within it. God rules in the statistical distributions of quantum mechanics. God rules over the statistical fluctuating of the nuclear fires of the sun. God sustains the universe and causes it to continue. God is waiting for men to come into fellowship with him. As has been recounted, God hates murder, God hates evil, God hates moral corruption.

God's apparent solution for evil is evil. Evil has within itself its own destruction by more evil. Examples of evil that have been presented herein are: the Spanish conquest of Mexico, the Spanish expeditions into the lands of North America, the indigenous people of California, and the people of the northwestern coast of North America.

In each of these examples there was widespread murder, killing of the innocent, homosexuality, cannibalism, and moral corruption extending into the sexual union of male and female man. All of these North American indigenous cultures have ceased to exist. There are very, very, few remaining individual people of these races of man. The remnant to a very great extent has mixed in with the Europeans and adopted European ways of living and European culture. The evil of those indigenous cultures has been destroyed by the evil of the conquerors. It still remains to be seen what will happen to the conquerors.

Now what is going on in all of this? The operations of God are a non-linear system within a non-linear system enfolded into itself an infinite number of times. We cannot predict what God will do or even think clearly of what God might do. God is unfathomable; His ways are unsearchable and past understanding. Nevertheless, we have been given God's moral law, examples of God's moral character, and we have been given a very meager understanding of God's magnificent righteousness.

We have been given the Bible and the Biblical accounts of what happened in the past to sundry doers of evil, and we have been given prophets who have spoken to us the words of God recorded in the Bible, warning us about evil doing, including moral sexual corruption. Finally, we have been given the words of Jesus Christ, the Son of God.

Looking at the statistics of these happenings, it is clear that morally corrupt cultures come to an end, sooner or later, probably when the stench gets so great God will no longer ignore it. No longer do we have in existence Greek, Roman, and many other peoples who once existed in the region of present Palestine, or past American nations. They are all gone. Most have for a long time been forgotten.

When the stench of moral corruption produced by those of mankind reaches a certain point, events happen. These events put an end to that particular stench. Then God waits patiently for righteous fruit of the revised order to happen.

Has the stench of American sexual corruption and stench of the murder of innocent little humans by the people of the United States become so great that God sends a new event to put an end to it?

Good examples of cultures disappearing in the presence of moral corruption have been presented. There is not necessarily a causality event here. Moral corruption is not necessarily a cause of cultural destruction. It is an enigma of a non-linear system within a non-linear system. We just observe that the cultures disappeared. God is omnipotent and rules supremely in His creation and in human civilization. When the stench is great, things happen.

Abraham, Lot, and Sodom

Consider now a written record concerning the person who is the father of believing saving faith in God, the man Abraham. Chapters 17 -19 of the Bible book of Genesis gives the account of Abraham dealing with the destruction of Sodom and Gomorrah.

The account is rather long and I choose not to quote it completely with all of the words of the Bible text. The reader is encouraged to read the account very, very carefully. Understand that the Apostle Paul says Abraham is the spiritual father of all Christian believers. We of faith in Jesus Christ understand that Abraham is our spiritual father. I will give a summary and paraphrase the account to present to you the extremely important information God gives to us.

When Abram is 99 years old God appears to him and says:

"I am God Almighty; Walk before me and be blameless. I will establish my covenant between Me and you"

This is the covenant of faith the Apostle Paul describes also given to Christian believers through faith in Jesus Christ. God changes Abram's name to Abraham, telling him he is to be the father of many nations; he is to be exceedingly fruitful.

This covenant is to be sealed with blood. As a sign of this covenant with Abraham, every male of Abraham's household is to be circumcised in the flesh of his foreskin. Abraham obeys, and that very day, Abraham has all the males in his household circumcised, including his son Ishmael, who became the father of the Arab nations.

Now the account says God appeared to Abraham by the oaks of Mamre. Mamre was in the southern hill country overlooking the beautiful well-watered plain below in the Jordan Valley. This was before the Lord God destroyed it.

Abraham is sitting by the door of his tent in the heat of the day and sees three men and runs to meet them. The account does not describe these three men, but they must have appeared very, very unique - as one of them is God in the form of a man, and the other two are angels of God, in the form of man. Abraham must have understood all this as he very quickly prepares a fellowship meal of meal cakes, choice calf, curds, and milk, and his guests ate before him.

God tells Abraham his wife is to have a son, even though she is old and has been barren all her life and is way past the age of child bearing. This child is to be a child of promise through which the covenant of faith is to continue, and through which all the nations of the earth will be blessed. Sarah hears from inside her tent and laughs, probably in astonishment.

As these men leave, God in the form of a man says, "Shall I not tell Abraham what I am going to do? Since Abraham will become a great and mighty nation, and so he will command his children and his household after him to keep the way of the Lord, by doing righteousness and justice, so the Lord may bring upon Abraham what He has spoke?"

Therefore, God told Abraham the stench from the cities of Sodom and Gomorrah is very great. The word sodomy comes from the name of this city of corruption, making this stench in the nostrils of God. It has got so bad that God says he came here to check it out. Abraham knows all about it as his nephew, Lot, lives in Sodom.

Then occurs a remarkable dialog between Abraham and God. This is the most extensive dialog between a man and God in the whole Bible. Abraham walks with God out to where the whole plain of the well-watered beautiful Jordan Valley can be seen far below. Abraham asks God, "Will You destroy the righteous with the wicked?" Yes, that is still the cry of mankind today. Will God destroy the righteous with the wicked? What a pain it is in our hearts to understand that the wicked must be destroyed. Our neighbors, our friends, our children, our nation, are to be destroyed because of wickedness. It hurts very much and we grieve.

We then have a remarkable dialog where Abraham starts with 50 people and eventually reduces it to ten, and then asks God, "Will you destroy Sodom and Gomorrah if yet ten righteous are found in the cities?" God listens to Abraham and says, no, He will not destroy the cities if ten righteous can be found in them.

Ten are not found, and the two angels are sent to destroy. They arrive as travelers at the Sodom city gate where Abraham's nephew, Lot, is sitting by the gate. Lot greets them and the angels say they will spend the night in the city square. Lot knows what will happen to them there and insists they come and stay with him.

These angels must have been very beautiful, handsome, young looking in the appearance of men, as the men of Sodom, young and old, arrive at Lot's door and demand the angels be given to them for that sexual activity that Sodom is known for and now bears its name. The angels blind the men of Sodom, frustrating the attack.

When dawn comes the angels physically grab Lot, his wife, and his two daughters, and drag them out of the city after much pleading with Lot to get out of there now and do it quickly. Lot cannot convince his prospective sons-in-law to leave as they think he is joking. Lot's wife cannot leave the city of corruption behind. She longs for the place and looks back. Her bones are left to be crusted with salt and made into a pillar by what became the Dead Sea, the most salty body of water on earth, and now has an awful offensive stench. Lot still pleads he be allowed to stay in a little city not too far away, and the angels comply with his request.

Here comes now what seems from the account to be perhaps a meteorite with fire and brimstone and the cities of the plains of Sodom are wiped out. Abraham probably hears the sound of it and rises early in the morning, and looks out over the plain, and observes the smoke of the place. I think Abraham was full of grief as he does not know what happened to his nephew, Lot; so Abraham pulls up his tent stakes and wanders south to encounter another trial of faith.

So here in the context of God establishing a covenant of faith with Abraham - this covenant of faith is to be extended to all believers through Jesus Christ - in this context God acts and destroys cities known for their sexual corruption. The question must be asked, "Why is sexual corruption so evil? Why must it be so destroyed? Why does God take this so seriously? After all, it is only a little romp in the grass hay for a little physical pleasure." Yes, indeed. Why?

Nephilim and Human DNA

Let me speculate a little. Scientific theories come and go. When new discoveries are made new theories are developed. Most scientists are seeking truth and try to build on the truth of the past. Sometimes, however, political forces get in the way and scientific discoveries are suppressed or lied about in the vein of political correctness, or the quandary of human greed.

There is a rather interesting account in the Bible in Genesis Chapter six which happened before the flood that covered the whole earth with water. Scholars and Christian theologians have struggled with it over the years. There is always the problem of translation and understanding the original meaning. Translators usually provide their own biased interpretation. From Genesis 6:1:

> "Now when it came about when men began to multiply on the face of the land, and daughters were born to them, that the sons of God saw that the daughters of men were beautiful; and they took for wives for themselves, whomever they chose."

The text goes on and in the context of this quotation, God says He will no longer strive with man. Man's days are to be terminated.

> "My Spirit shall not strive with man forever, because he also is flesh, nevertheless his days shall be one hundred and twenty years."

Something called Nephilim showed up on the earth when the sons of God bred the daughters of men. This breeding produced renowned men, mighty men, famous men of old. Cross breading of sub-species and inbreed lines can produce animals of great vigor. The context seems to indicate this may be what happened here. Because then wickedness, subsequently, became very great. The whole context of this account is evil and wickedness, the thoughts of man then being only evil continually.

God was grieved He had made man and decided to wipe them out. But He gave them another 120 years, as Noah somehow found favor with God. One hundred twenty years later after Noah had finished building a huge ark boat, and then had the ark ready for his voyage on the flood waters, God sent the flood to destroy all of mankind.

Bible scholars and theologians have struggled with this Nephilim passage for years. In our day scientists have said the genetic DNA (a molecular coding system in each cell of flesh which determines everything of what a man is) of man has about four percent of it identical to that of the Neanderthals. DNA of other humanoid species is also apparently in the human DNA. Neanderthals are an ape like humanoid species that archeologists say may have existed until maybe 30,000 to 50,000 years ago. Denisovans are another humanoid species perhaps from Asia which also have disappeared but left DNA in humans, especially in Melanesian and Australian aborigines. There may be DNA of other ancient humanoid species mixed in with humans also.

Allow me to postulate a possibility. The text does not define daughters of men or sons of God. Let me postulate the sons of God as meaning the humanoid Adam line from the Garden of Eden, and the daughters of men as females of other humanoid species, maybe Neanderthals, or Denisovans, or other. So here we have, potentially, bestiality taking place. The sons of God are maybe breeding animal species of humanoids making cross bread men of renown, yes, and very mighty men, and apparently, from the context of the text, very evil men.

Cross breading produces great animal vigor, especially when cross breeding two selected, highly inbred animal species. I once aspired to be a bear hunter by hunting with hound dogs. I acquired a bitch of renowned bear hunting capability, a Plott Hound, from someone in North Carolina. The family pet was a large beautiful black and white collie. I gave instructions to my wife to be sure and keep them apart, but as things will happen, during a Bible study conducted by my wife, the collie and the Plott Hound got together. Well, here came a litter of pups. I did not think the pups would make it as bear hunting hounds so I gave them away, one to my sister and her family, and one to a neighbor.

At the time I lived in an upscale neighborhood of one acre minimum size lots in Los Altos Hills, California. Our family's house was on a ridge top, and our neighbor's house was about one-half mile away across a valley-like bowl to the northwest. The neighbor tied his dog to a wire line maybe 200 feet long, and from my house I could see and hear that dog going up and down and back and forth on that line, making a huge noise which I heard real loud from ½ mile away, day after day. That dog did it all day long and never tired. Those crossbred dogs were unbelievably strong and vigorous. My sister's dog was so strong it was almost impossible for even a strong grown man to hold it back when on a leash.

Given the context of the account and the vigorousness of the result, this apparent cross breeding of humanoids, one a very pure DNA line from the Garden of Eden, produced not only men of renown, but men of great strength and great evil, fighting and killing one another.

After the flood, after God destroyed all of this mixed human race except the line of Noah, his three sons and their wives, God made a very strong provision of law against murder, saying that every murderer of man, man or beast, must be in turn be killed by man. So God said enough is enough and with great grief, decided man must be terminated by a flood of water.

With this historical context and the resulting evil, we can perhaps understand why God so hates bestiality, sodomy, fornication, and all forms of sexual misconduct. It is destructive to man, destroys man, and makes man prone to do great evil, killing, robbing, hating, and destroying one another.

God hates evil. God hates fornication. God hates sodomy.

Wrath on False Teachers

From the Book of Jude, verses 4-7:

"For certain persons have crept in unnoticed, those who were long beforehand marked out for this condemnation, ungodly persons who turn the grace of God into licentiousness and deny our only master and Lord, Jesus Christ. Now I desire to remind you, through you know all things once for all that the Lord, after saving a people out of the land of Egypt, subsequently destroyed those who did not believe. And angels who did not keep their own domain, but abandoned their proper abode, he has kept in eternal bonds under darkness for the judgment of the great day, just as Sodom and Gomorrah and the cities around them, since they in the same way as these indulged in gross immorality and went after strange flesh, are exhibited as an example in undergoing the punishment of eternal fire."

Presbyterian Church, USA

As stated, I grew up in the home of a pastor who devoted his life to the Kingdom of Jesus Christ and he worked hard to bring into the Kingdom new believers for fellowship with Jesus. He then taught the communicant believers a lifestyle of spiritual growth with Jesus. I made my profession of faith in Jesus Christ, in my father's denomination, the Presbyterian Church, USA, and became a member of that Church.

Now in the year of our Lord, 2015, the General Assembly of that church denomination, adopted the homosexual lifestyle as fit and proper for church leaders and through them, the communicant believers. What ugly, horrible corruption. As this previous passage from the book of Jude proclaims, there is a special place in the eternal bonds of darkness, in the dark black fires of eternal hell, for false teachers. That denomination has now adopted this false teaching as the gospel to be preached and adopted in the Presbyterian Church, USA.

Let us all remember the gospel of Jesus Christ is for sinners. Jesus said He came to earth to save sinners, not the righteous. Sinners are welcome at the foot of the cross of Jesus. By faith in Jesus, repentant sinners from among those of man are brought into the Kingdom of God, including those who have in the past engaged in gross sexual immorality, theft, lying, adultery, and even murder.

But woe to those Christian leaders who teach that moral corruption of the flesh, or living in any other lifestyle of crime, is acceptable or appropriate for a believer, and as such, may be practiced by a communicant of the church. All the elders, presbyters, ministers, Stated Clerks, officers of the Presbyteries, officers of the General Assembly, etc., of that denomination are now under that wrath of God, especially that horrible wrath which is especially put on false teachers.

When Jesus addressed the false teachers of his days on earth, He said to them in Mathew 24:33,

> **"You serpents, you brood of vipers, how will you escape the sentence of hell?"**

Yes, indeed, judgment is coming on the Presbyterian Church, USA, and all other denominations, that teach, advocate, or tolerate, homosexual corruption as an appropriate lifestyle for Christian leaders and then for believers and potential believers.

Jesus told a parable about a rich man and a beggar who begged at his gate (Luke 16:19-31):

> "Now there was a rich man, and he habitually dressed in purple and fine linen, joyously living in splendor every day. And a poor man named Lazarus was laid at his gate, covered with sores, and longing to be fed from the rich man's table; besides, even the dogs were coming and licking his sores. Now the poor man died and was carried away by the angels to Abraham's bosom; and the rich man also died and was buried. In Hades he lifted up his eyes, being in torment and saw Abraham far away and Lazarus in his bosom. And he cried out and said , 'Father Abraham have mercy on me, and send Lazarus

so that he may dip the tip of his finger in water and cool off my tongue, for I am in agony in this flame.' But Abraham said, 'Child remember, that during your life you received your good things, and likewise Lazarus bad things; now he is being comforted here, and you are in agony. And besides all this, between us and you is a great chasm fixed, so that those who wish to come over from here to you will not be able, and that none may cross over from there to us.' And he said, 'Then I beg you, father, that you send him to my father's house - for I have five brothers - in order that he may warn them, so that they will not also come to this place of torment.' But Abraham said, 'they have Moses and the Prophets; let them hear them.' But he said, 'No, father Abraham, but if someone goes to them from the dead, they will repent!' But he said to him, 'If they do not listen to Moses and the Prophets, they will not be persuaded even if someone rises from the dead.' "

Jesus in this parable gives us inkling about hell. Jesus in His parable intended to communicate that even if one rises from the dead, unbelievers will still not believe. Believing in Jesus as Lord of one's life is a profound thing, and even if someone rises from the dead, unbelievers will still not believe.

But the description of hell is very clear. It is a dark, black, fiery, very hot place in which the inhabitants are in terrible torment. False teachers, those that lead man astray and corrupt the fellowship between man and God, are destined to spend eternity in torment in this fiery black place of hell, even though they are respected leaders of the Church on earth.

Jesus' Parables on the Kingdom of Heaven

Jesus told another parable about the Kingdom of God.

"He presented another parable to them, saying, "The kingdom of heaven is like a mustard seed, which a man took and sowed in his field; and this is smaller than all seeds, but when it is full grown, it is larger than the garden plants and becomes a tree, so that the birds of the air come and nest in its branches."

In the context of Jesus telling this parable, Jesus told several other parables some of which He interpreted; thus we understand a little what these symbols in the parables mean. Understand, mustard is not a tree and mustard seed is not the smallest of all seeds. Therefore, a mustard seed growing into a tree indicates a non-expected thing, a corruption. Mustard is a small green plant with yellow flowers that grow uniformly in a beautiful field of green and yellow. A tree is a symbol of a power structure. The birds are carrion birds, ugly black vultures that roost and nest in dead snag trees, agents of Satan, and appear to rule over the fields of carrion below them, searching for the remains of victims of the vicissitudes of life.

Jesus is telling about His own Church! Yes, what Jesus intends for His Church is a beautiful fellowship of lovely Christians living uniformly together in love, like a beautiful uniform field of green plants with yellow flowers. Instead the visible church that comes up is a power structure ruled over by corrupt men in high places feeding on the carrion. That is exactly what has happened to the Presbyterian Church, USA!

Of course, that has also happened to other denominations and other so called churches over the ages. But here is a very clear example in our time of Church leaders who profess they are Christians and true worshipers of God instead corrupt the visible church with false teaching and lead many astray down into hell. Again, God has a very special place in hell for such false teachers, those who lead man astray and corrupt the fellowship of man with his God.

In the same context Jesus told another parable, Matthew 13:33:

> "He spoke another parable to them, 'The kingdom of heaven is like leaven, which a woman took and hid in three pecks of flour until it was all leavened.' "

Unfortunately this parable has been very much misunderstood and misinterpreted. For understanding, examine the symbols. The Bible is its own interpreter. Leaven is a symbol of evil and corruption.

It has been used to represent that many times in the Bible. The NAS translators have called the measure of the amount of the flour, three pecks. What the original has is three measures of meal, the same expression as used in the Temple of the Jews, as the fellowship grain offering. So, three measures of meal symbolize the fellowship offering - the fellowship relationship of believing worshipers with God. Pastor Ray Stedman in his writings has said use of the word women in this context is a symbol of misplaced authority. That is very correct. The interpretation of the parable then is - leaders in the kingdom of God, misplaced corrupt leaders, improper leaders, corrupt the fellowship of the believers in the Kingdom of God, and the corruption spreads through the whole church organization like leaven spreads through the whole amount of a batch of dough.

Wow! That is again just exactly what the corrupt leaders of the Presbyterian Church, USA, are doing to their followers. Jesus has laid out what corrupt leaders in the church do. They destroy the sweet fellowship of believers with God, and replace it with moral corruption which leads down into hell!

Jesus Pronounces Woe on False Teachers

Jesus gives us a rather complete description of corrupt leaders in the Kingdom of God in the 23rd chapter of the book of Matthew. He said the scribes and Pharisees have seated themselves in the seat of Moses. That is, they have presumed themselves to be the leaders of the Jewish religion. These leaders then exercise the prerogatives of the leadership, receive respectful greetings from each other and their followers, and give themselves respectful names.

Jesus pronounces woe unto them. This same woe must be placed on false teachers of our day. That is very appropriate pronouncement as the leaders of present day false teaching church denominations do the same as the false teachers of Jesus' day. Seven woes were pronounced by Jesus on false teachers. Here I present a very similar pattern of seven woes with the same thrust and meaning as that of Jesus on false teaching.

ONE: Woe on you false teachers, blind guides, hypocrites, for you shut off the Kingdom of Heaven in your parishioners' faces. You do not enter the Kingdom yourself and you shut off those entering to go in. Yes, false teachers shut off the great benefits of the Kingdom of God to people who want to go in and who want and desire to come to know and enjoy fellowship with God. And you shut them out by your false teaching.

TWO: Woe on you false teachers, blind guides, hypocrites, for you travel on land and sea to search for new proselytes. You send missionaries all over the world, spend lots of money all over seeking proselytes, yes, even for a single proselyte, and make him as much a son of hell as you.

THREE: Woe on you false teachers, blind guides, hypocrites, for you lie. You take the oath of your office promising to keep and hold forth the historical doctrines of your denomination when you become an office holder, but you cross your fingers like a child does when he does not want to tell the truth. In your mode of operation, if you cross your mental fingers when you swear an oath, you do not really mean your oath and just lie. Like the scribes and Pharisees, Jesus said if they swear by the Temple it means nothing, but if they swear by the gold of the Temple, then it means something. You false denominational teachers and leaders do the same. If you have reservations about the sworn statement you are about to make, you think in your mind, this statement is archaic thinking and doctrine, so I do not have to really believe the writings of the Church fathers. So then you lie with a false sworn oath and think you do not have to believe the silly fundamental doctrines of your denomination. You blind ones of man! You swear an oath in front of the throne of God, and to Him who sits on the throne! You think there is no consequence to swear a false oath before God when you assume an office in His visible Church? Yes, your destiny is black fiery hell as a false teacher!

FOURTH: Woe on you false teachers, blind guides, hypocrites, you who go and collect tithes and offerings and neglect justice and mercy.

You create for yourselves and then vote in the assembly for yourselves high salaries and marvelous pensions and sell your empty churches for big bucks and spend the money on yourselves, neglecting justice and faithfulness to your oath. Woe on you, you who strain out gnats and swallow camels. Anybody who does not play along with your corruption, you throw out of the church.

FIFTH: Woe on you false teachers, blind guides, hypocrites, for you wash yourselves on the outside and attempt to look very clean and nice on the outside in fine clothes and robes, but inside you are full of robbery and self-indulgence. You blind guides, first clean your inner self so your outer self can reflect truth and righteousness that comes from within.

SIX: Woe on you false teachers, blind guides, hypocrites, for you have trained yourself to act righteously, but deep within, you are unclean and full of rottenness, as rotten as dead men bones. Your hearts are unclean; your hearts have not been washed by the Holy Spirit of God. You conduct yourself before men just as an actor on a stage, appearing righteous, but inwardly, within your heart, you are full of all manner of evil, rottenness, a stench in the nostrils of God.

SEVENTH: Woe on you false teachers, blind guides, hypocrites, for you build monuments to those you have destroyed in the past, built church buildings and dedicate them, and say we would not have in the past persecuted those who wanted to reform the Church. Hereby you testify against yourself.

As Jesus said, you serpents, you brood of vipers, how are you to escape being sentenced to hell?

Meeting of False Leaders

My father told me of a time he went to a Presbytery meeting in San Jose, California. My father had retired from the PCUSA. In that denomination the clergy are not members of some local church, but remain a member of Presbytery, a body consisting of the pastors and

Ruling Elders of a group of churches. The request came up to transfer the membership of Rev. A John Doe to another Presbytery. My father stood up and made the motion that Rev. A John Doe not be transferred in good standing, because as my father said, he had heard him preach in the Palo Alto Presbyterian Church, where Rev. A. John Doe was the Pastor, that Jesus Christ was mistaken when He said He would rise from the dead.

Normally my father was ignored by the dominate liberals in Presbytery and this motion would die for lack of a second on the motion. But at that particular meeting, to my father's surprise and joy, a Ruling Elder in the back of the assembly seconded the motion to amend. Now according to the rules of Presbytery, the motion had to be discussed and acted upon. So one Pastor after another rose up and said, "We all know Rev. A. John Doe, and he is a very fine fellow."

Yes, indeed, a very fine fellow, a false teacher destined for the black fires of hell. Needless to say, the motion to transfer him in good standing passed by all the, construed to be, liberal majority in the Presbytery. My father was surprised by the number of those present in the meeting who voted with the minority as to not transfer in good standing. At that time there was still a remnant in that denomination that loved and followed the Lord Jesus in truth, at least in the San Jose Presbytery.

I say to all those believers in Jesus Christ who still remain in that denomination, come out, shake the dust off your feet, give that denomination over to Satan for discipline, and leave. What fellowship can truth have with error or false teaching? The moral corruption of homosexuality will absolutely destroy any effectiveness whatsoever for the Kingdom of God in that denomination. If you remain, you will be under the damnation and woe pronounced on false teachers by Jesus Himself.

Now understand me. There are many false teachers out there. There are other denominations on the same corrupt path as the PCUSA. I pick out the PCUSA for particular notice as my spirit is stirred up about the PCUSA, because I grew up in that denomination, and made my profession of faith in Jesus Christ in that denomination. I am very grieved for that denomination and grieved for the people still in it. Other relatives of mine have served in that denomination and some are still there. Its leaders have become what my father called a mutual admiration society, a corrupt leaven for destruction, with grievous wolves among them, according to Acts Chapter 20.

All that terrible woe Jesus pronounced on false teachers surely applies to the PCUSA, as descriptions of these modern false teachers in the PCUSA, are the same as Jesus gave for those false teachers of his day. They love to be greeted in the market place and given greetings as Reverend so and so and sing the praises of one another and declare to each other, we are all very fine fellows here, indeed. They can now greet each other and feel really good in and about themselves and say to each other, "What fine fellows we are, look what great things we have done for those poor persecuted homosexuals." Yes, indeed, and join them on their sin trip into hell, both in this world and the fiery hot black one of torment in the next.

The Apostle Paul declared in Romans, the 1st chapter, that homosexuality is the curse of God on unbelief. That is exactly what has happened. Widespread unbelief among the leadership, pastors, and parishioners in the PCUSA has come home to roost. Under the wrath of God, the PCUSA has received its due consequence of sexual corruption - how so very, very, sad. It fills me with grief.

We should not be surprised by all this. Jesus told another parable in the same context as the parables of the sower, the mustard seed, and the woman and the meal (Matthew 13:24):

> "Jesus presented another parable to them, saying, "The kingdom of heaven may be compared to a man who sowed good seed in his field. But while his men were sleeping, his enemy came and sowed tares among the wheat, and went away. But when the wheat sprouted and bore grain, then the tares became evident also. The slaves of the landowner came and said to him, 'Sir did you not sow

> good seed in your field? How then does it have tares?' And he said to them, 'an enemy has done this!' The slaves said to him, 'Do you want us, then to go and gather them up?' But he said, 'No, for while you are gathering them up, you may uproot the wheat with them. Allow both to grow together until the harvest; and in the time of the harvest I will say to the reapers, 'First gather up the tares, and bind them in bundles to burn them up; but gather the wheat into my barn. ' "

Jesus explained this parable to his disciples so we do not have to analyze much to understand the meaning. The sower is Jesus. The field is the world. The good seed is the sons of the Kingdom, and the tares are the sons of evil. The enemy who sowed is the devil, the harvest is the end of the age, and the reapers are the angels. At the end of the age the tares are gathered up and burned. Jesus will send forth his angels and they will gather up out of his Kingdom all stumbling blocks and those who commit lawlessness and throw them into the hot furnace of fire where there is weeping and gnashing of teeth.

Yes, that is the picture of the visible Church of Jesus Christ. Tares are the weeds in the visible church. The righteous symbolized by the wheat have been washed in their hearts. They develop together with the wicked stumbling blocks and false teachers among them. As the washed hearts and the unwashed hearts develop together, gradually one can distinguish between then. Jesus said, "By their fruit you will know them." Fruits are manifested in the flesh of the body in the real world. Observe wicked fruits and be warned. At the end of the age the unwashed are gathered together and cast into the furnace of fiery hell.

The fruit of homosexuality is corruption and wickedness. The practice of sexual corruption becomes obvious to the world. Repentance and confession of sin must occur or such practitioners will join the other unwashed in that terrible fire of hell.

After Jesus presented the understanding of this parable, He gave two more simple, very short parables that have been very misunderstood and quite misanalysed. From Matthew 13:44:

"The kingdom of heaven is like a treasure hidden in the field, which a man found and hid, and from joy over it he goes and sells all that he has and buys that field."

"Again, the kingdom of heaven is like a merchant seeking fine pearls, and upon finding one pearl of great value, he went and sold all he had and bought it."

Most commentators on the Bible interpret the treasure in the field as the nation Israel. But the Bible is its own interpreter. Jesus has provided the interpretation of the symbols in the previous parables. The field is the world. Jesus' universal invisible Church of all the washed hearts must be the treasure as it hides out in the world and is not obvious. The man in the parable is Jesus. The Holy Spirit of Jesus finds those who belong to Jesus as His own and washes them and then hides them back out into the world. In joy, Jesus gives all that he has and goes out and buys the world of believers by the shedding of his precious blood. The treasure represents the saved people of the believing universal Church of Jesus Christ, not tribal Israel.

The second parable seems always to be misinterpreted by Bible commentators. The man in this whole series of seven parables is Jesus, but in this parable Jesus introduces the merchant. Who is the merchant? Jesus cannot be represented by a merchant. Jesus never characterized himself as a businessman, that is, one who buys and sells. So in this parable we have a merchant businessman wandering around the world looking for pearls he can buy and sell. The Jews apparently never considered pearls as jewels or any pearls as being especially valuable. Pearls were a gentile thing of the Greeks and Romans.

Let me suggest to you that the merchant represents the individual seeker of truth and righteousness. As we of this race of man wander around in the world and pass through the vicissitudes, trials, troubles, and tribulation of life, we deep down within us have a hunger after truth, beauty, and meaning; yes, we want to find pearls. Yes, we seek the meaning and the truth of life. So we look over and examine many sundry pearls encountered throughout life and sometimes we buy and sell. But yes, then through the grace of God, we find Jesus! We come to love Jesus. We become heart washed and we find that one and only pearl of very great price, Jesus, the King of Kings, the Lord of Lords! We believers sell all we have and we buy Jesus. Jesus becomes the only thing of real meaning in our whole life!

So now to complete the whole parable sequence in this book of Matthew, consider the last of the seven parables Jesus told (Matthew 13:47-50):

> "Again the kingdom of heaven is like a dragnet cast into the sea, and gathering up of every kind; and when it was filled, they drew it up on the beach; and they sat down and gathered the good into containers, but the bad they threw away. So it will be at the end of the age, the angels will come forth and take out the wicked from among the righteous, and throw them into the furnace of fire; in that place there will be weeping and gnashing of teeth."

This concludes Jesus' sequence of seven parables and this particular last one needs no further interpretation. The end of everything on earth is very, very clear. The wicked are thrown away and the righteous are gathered into Jesus beautiful, magnificent heaven.

ELEVEN

Alliance Fourfold Teaching

In contrast to the false teachers who preach another gospel are the teachings of Christian Churches and organizations that have their own variation on the presentation of the Gospel of Jesus Christ.

As an example so to show fourfold teaching, let's compare it with the teachings of Christian and Missionary Alliance. Reviewed is the information about what their founder called, "Fourfold Gospel", on it's website as of September 2020.

This Alliance description of the Christian Gospel of Jesus Christ according to their understanding, reflects a fourfold approach and is somewhat similar in approach to the fourfold presentation of the full four realm creation of the universe as herein given. Founder Simpson understood a fourfold structure of man. He put his own fourfold stamp on it, calling it savior, sanctifier, healer, and King Jesus.

If you think about it for a while, you will understand that what Alliance presents is savior of the body, sanctifier of the soul, healer of the spirit (which gives direction to the soul which has control over the body), and then as a forth, the eventual millennial Kingdom of Jesus Christ. Now Simpson put his own theological stamp on the whole thing to promote his gospel. He has made a very important contribution to understanding man. Yes, man is composed of body, soul, spirit, and heart --- body of flesh in the reality of space-time, soul in the huge realm of all souls, man's own spirit in the vast realm of all spirits, and the ruling kingship of the heart of man wherein direction of life is made from that inner essence of mankind, the heart.

The first statement, "Jesus Christ as our Savior", reflects that our transformed bodies are indeed to be preserved complete in the Eternity of the Heavens as having been saved.

The second statement, "Jesus Christ is our Sanctifier", reflects the process that occurs in our souls as we grow and become more Christ like during the process of living out our life. As our minds as part of our souls (The soul consists of the mind, will, and emotions.) processes the experiences of life, we Christians become more and more committed to obedience to the thoughts and commands of Christ, so we are to become sanctified. This process occurs in our souls in the second realm. Souls have been defined as the second realm in this four realm understanding.

The third statement, "Christ is our Healer", reflects the power of the Holy Spirit to create healing anywhere in man's whole being. Miracles that occur when it seems that the physical laws of the universe have been suspended so as to create the change in the status of the body so that it is healed, can very well, in most cases, just be as an extension of the ideas herein of this treatise, wherein God picks the event in the distribution of possibilities, where, of course, the possibility of a complete healing event exits in the potential whole distribution of possibilities. So God is just picking the event in potential space-time possibilities where the person is rapidly healed.

Jesus often did something which at the time it occurred is called a miracle, but in our modern days is something that could happen when done by medical professionals given adequate time. What Jesus did was to control time and just speed it up or slow it down. Speeding up as through controlling time is a principal discussed in this book.

The fourth statement, "Jesus Christ is Our Coming King", reflects the understanding that Jesus rules in our lives, (However, founder Simson believed it was to come in the Millennium), that Jesus rules over His universe. However, it is in our hearts where the rule of life occurs.

Now consider the process of the treatise herein presented in the progression of the Christian life. The Apostle Peter was a fisherman when Jesus employed him for ministry. A fisherman catches fish. So Peter has the Christ given apostolic ministry of catching men for the Kingdom. The transformation of a person of mankind into being a believer in Jesus Christ occurs in the heart of the being. The heart is washed clean or in some biblical statements say given a new heart. The heart is cleaned, renewed, or made new, and the person is now a child of God. This is a binary operation --- a new Christian either receives a new clean heart, or the old wicked evil prone heart remains --- either one or the other. There is nothing in between. It must be one or the other. This is the first event in the Christian life and occurs in the fourfold realm of the heart.

The next step in the process of the Christian life is acquiring knowledge about the Christian life and understanding of what the Christian life and thinking is all about. The Apostle Paul was a professor, a teacher, and explainer in his original Jewish profession of teaching and explaining. Then Jesus directly appeared to him on the Damascus Road, captured him by grace, and told him now he was to be a professor of truth in the Kingdom of God. This activity occurs in the soul realm, the third of the fourfold operations of Christian life.

So these two types of ministry operations in the early formation of Christ's Universal Church for the first approximately forty years after Jesus resurrection, created the Church. These operations are similar to what go on in the individual Christian life. First a washed renewed heart and then knowledge of truth --- that truth of the Gospel of the Lord Jesus Christ.

Now forty years is a biblical time of testing or trial, often describing an all-encompassing defining event. The Jews were given forty years to repent and have remorse over their crucifixion of the Son of God.

Then came for the Jews and for the Church what I call a "Jerusalem Event". At about the year 70 AD the Romans came and destroyed Jerusalem, and scattered the Jews and Christians all over the earth --- a terrible ugly murderous process that seemingly destroyed everything dear to believers. Similarly, something like this often happens in the Christian's life. Things seem to be progressing properly and then an ugly arrives. Spouse wants a divorce, business decisions causes the loss of assets; thieves, crooks, do-gooders or whatnot, take away cherished things and destroy ones comfortable life, and ruin everything, or take most everything away. Yes, something bad happens --- a period of testing and trial that God is working out in the Christian life.

After the destruction of the Jews and the Jerusalem Event, the Church went through a period of false teaching. The Bible book of the Apostle Jude deals with this ministry against false teachers. False teachers get identified by the occurrence of sins of the flesh in their lives. These sins are committed in the body of flesh --- in the real life of the false teacher, or in a teacher concerned only for the money available to a Christian teacher.

In the early Church there occurred a period of approximately twenty years of this extensive false teaching and turmoil in the Church. After this occurs the time of emphasis of the ministry of the Apostle John. John was mending nets when Jesus called him to ministry of being an Apostle. John had the very important ministry of mending spirts, fixing spirits, healing spirits, with an emphasis on the fruits of the spirt --- love, joy, peace, kindness, goodness, and patience. The Apostle John lived to a very old age, maybe even to about the year 117 AD. My own thinking, with no biblical or historical proof, is that Jesus called him home, and John never saw death like did the prophet Elijah, but was transformed.

Jesus responded to Peter when Peter asked Him at the beach barbeque after Jesus' resurrection, "What about him", meaning John. Jesus responded, "If I wish him to remain until I come, what is that to you." Remember John was the disciple that Jesus loved in a very special way.

Thus understand the fourfold apostolic ministry emphasis in the early Church and how it developed. First twenty years of Peter type ministry, then twenty years of Paul type ministry, then the Jerusalem event, then twenty years of Jude type ministry, and then twenty years and much more and continuing of a John type healing ministry.

So here we have presented the Apostolic fourfold realm sequence of the creation and full life type development of the Universal Christian Church on the Earth--- heart and soul, and then body and spirit.   Similarly, is the individual Christian life sequence --- heart washing, soul building, trials and tribulations, resisting and fighting false teaching including sins of the body of flesh, mending and growth of the spirit.   Call this whole path of the Christian life the, "Apostolic Fourfold Realm Life".

Twelve

Man and Wife Joined into One

Let's go back and consider again the creation of man so to expand on these concepts, receive understanding on paired monogamous marriage, and bring the observations to a conclusion.

From Genesis 2:18:

"Then the Lord God said, "It is not good for the man to be alone; I will make a helper suitable for Him."

Then the Lord God had the man examine all the plants and animals He had made. He asked the man to give them names, but none was suitable for a helper.

Then in verses 21-24:

"So the Lord God caused a deep sleep to fall upon the man, and he slept; then He took one of his ribs and closed up the flesh at that place. The Lord God fashioned into a women the rib which he had taken from the man and brought her to the man.
The man said, 'This is now bone of my bones,
And flesh of my flesh;
She shall be called Woman,
Because she was taken out of Man.'

For this reason a man shall leave his father and mother, and be joined to his wife; and they shall become one flesh."

From this account we observe some very fascinating things:

Man was divided into two beings, yet same bones and flesh

The woman taken out of the man

Man is joined back together when he leaves his father and mother and joins his wife.

What do we make of this? Jesus quoted this statement when some Pharisees and Jewish legal experts were quizzing Him about divorce (Matthew 19:5). Jesus then added,

> "So they are no longer two, but one flesh. What God has joined together, let no man separate."

There is for us some really profound meaning to this. Man (meaning both male and female) is conceived, is born, grows up, is taught, is trained by parents, and is immersed in the tribe or culture in which he lives. Then one finds a wife or husband.

Male Man and Female Man Joined Into One

God says the two become one. There is deep spiritual significant meaning here for us. How is it that two are joined together and become one? Physically, we know that is impossible. Thus the meaning to be conveyed is that the two are joined together in their spirits. From the realm fourfold understanding I am conveying to you, spiritual union means the cup of the man's spirit holds the woman's spirit, and the cup of the woman's spirit holds the man's spirit. To keep things clear in the verbal description of this wonder, understand that masculine humans are male man, and women are female man. So when male man and female man are joined together we again have complete man.

With this understanding, the sexual union of male and female man has a much deeper meaning than most theologians and philosophers over the centuries have provided and given to mankind.

Using the four realm fourfold concept, from the shadowed picture presented by the tabernacle, it is understood that the heart realm is deep within the spirit realm. The spirit overshadows the heart. The tabernacle/ark shadow picture indicates the washed-clean purified believing heart receives and thus contains the right correct thrust of God's rule and law, continuous daily spiritual manna food input from God for developing heart life, and confidence from God that heart belongs to God, is possessed by God. Thus two hearts that have been joined and washed-clean with purification share each other's goals and understandings - the function of the heart. Conflict over the direction and operation of life attenuate and even disappear as the two hearts continuously entwine.

Again, consider the existential view derived from the four realm picture of understanding. From the shadow picture example of the tabernacle; the room of the soul is the gateway to the room of the spirit. When two spirits are joined together, being mutually shared, there is communication between the respective spirits to the respective souls. The soul of each washed-clean purified heart person receives understanding light for the soul as represented by the tabernacle lamp, mental food like information input for the soul as represented by the bread of the presence, and power for prayer generation by the paired souls as represented by the smoke of the alter of incense. All of these together have communication with the respective spirits, and so receive similar motivation from the believing washed-clean purified hearts through the spirits into the believing thinking souls. So mental light, mental food, and mental prayer generation, the functionality of the soul, with help from God, creates feedback. This feedback occurs through the washed-clean purified hearts into the spirits and back into the souls.

The soul has the memory bank that keeps track of the input received from God. When the two spirits are merged or share each other, the input from the heart of each is filtered so that the memory banks of each start to receive recollections of shared memories, the memories reinforce each other, and close fellowship brings the souls mutually together. This makes for a pair of man, male and female, to have the same or very similar motivations. The decisions of life such as how to raise and discipline children, make decisions on how life is to be lived, where life is to be lived, who to fellowship with in life, and who to not fellowship with, are mutually made.

This all comes about because of reinforcing, intense sexual pleasure and ecstasy that occurs and binds them totally together within an ongoing married committed relationship. The ongoing deep merged flesh/spiritual sexual experience, often repeated, reinforces the bonding between the male man and the female man. This grows and grows so conflicts, trials, troubles, and vicissitudes of life can be handled.

Trials and troubles occur in the realm of the flesh of the body. The soul processes these inputs. The spirit absorbs the inputs and then communicates them to the heart wherein the spiritual food from God, the rules and understanding from God, and the knowledge that both the male and the female of man belong to God, creates feedback to the spirit. The spirit then feeds such to the soul so the souls can come to mutual understandings as to what decisions to make, and what is to be done in real physical life.

All of this is complex and is really never thought through by the partners. It just happens. Humans have been given a genetic code so the body and soul grow together and develop as life goes on from conception, to birth, to maturation. The spirit breathed into the embryo at conception by God, overshadows the infant heart, that most inner essence of the new man person. Then the life of little new man grows and grows into maturity throughout all of life on into adulthood. Then a mate is to be found.

Satanic Destruction of the Sexual Relationship

The drives developed within man life, mandated by the genetic code provided by God, and then produced by the body and soul; cause a seeking of a sexual partner. Life of man is never thoroughly complete until a sexual partner is discovered. Then if corruption has occurred so the sexual partner is quite confused or does not have a washed purified heart, Satan has a field day setting about a process to destroy that person and make that person a candidate for hell and death as Satan so powerfully desires. This is why God so abhors fornication and other sexual corruption in man.

God is looking for fellowship with man. God has provided a way for fallen, corrupted man to come to fellowship with God. The way is to come to the Man resurrected from the dead, the Son of God, Jesus. Confess with the mouth Jesus as Lord of one's life and believe in the heart that God raised Jesus from the dead. Then the Spirit of God comes to live in the man spirit, male and female, and the Spirit of God washes and cleans and purifies that believer's heart. This is a new beginning.

The Holy Spirit of God then starts a process of living within the man spirit so the heart and soul are connected with the mediating, mending influence of the Spirit of God within the man spirit. Healing then can occur where the brokenness caused by past corruption can be fixed. Male and female man with both having purified hearts, can build their relationships together. If only one of the pair is heart-purified the development is more complex, but the Apostle Paul has given guidance as to how to proceed. The washed one is not to leave the relationship if the unwashed one consents to stay, for then the washed heart has the opportunity to bring the unwashed one to knowledge of Jesus as Savior, so that the unwashed one can be washed, and any children of the relationship blessed. But if the unwashed one wants to leave the relationship, Paul says to let that one go.

Fixing and mending past corruption is not easy. The marvelous thing is that often the fixed, mended person becomes much more of a lover of God than the man person who never experienced much past corruption. This is a mystery. The experience of God moving into one's spirit and fixing the corruption gives a very strong confidence in the power of God to fix things, so making that person highly motivated to tell others of the experience. All man is corrupt. However, it seems those who have grown up in fellowship with God do not seem to have the same fire in their bellies to go out and seek for healing the lost ones for God, as those who recently have become saved.

Procreation of Children

Nevertheless, the sexual bond between two washed purified hearts gives the pair great strength to create a strong, safe place where new additional man children can be procreated. Yes, to bring many new man (children) unto God for fellowship. This ultimately is the goal of strong exquisite sexual love; it is to provide many, very many, new man for fellowship with God and for the manifest of Glory to God.

Satan has worked overtime to corrupt this relationship. There is intense ecstatic pleasure in the sexual union act. This captures the soul and feeds the spirit with beautiful ecstasy. Consequently, Satan has used that experience, which God intended to bind couples together in strong close spiritual communion so as to become one, to corrupt and destroy the fellowship relationship of male and female man with God.

To a great extent our present American occidental culture has been initiated and inherited from the ancient Greek civilization. Those Greeks invented gods to give their culture meaning and guidance. A huge part of the Greek culture was devoted to gods who would be worshiped in the god's temple by engaging the temple prostitutes. Whores, gigolos, and others of a sexual deviant manner operated near the temples. Thus fornication became the main lifestyle of the whole of Greek culture and was the norm for most everyone throughout that culture.

One might ask, "Why does Satan work overtime to destroy the intimate sexual union between male man and female man by erotic fornication just for the physical genital pleasure of it rather than have the ecstasy of close spiritual union?" The answer is that Satan's goal is to destroy man and destroy man's fellowship with the Almighty Lord God. Satan is very successful at destroying that fellowship by side tracking man into activities of only genital stimulation. This is tragedy indeed.

History of Fornication in Greek Culture

Cathy Gaca, in her most excellent, very scholarly book, has provided a history of fornication in ancient Greek culture.[12] The ideas of the following three paragraphs to a great extent are taken from the conclusions of her writings with a little modification to build my points for understanding Greek fornicating culture.

Cathy concludes the Apostle Paul's Christian writings in the Bible, the ideas of sexual morality and the resulting social change, are revolutionary in their formulation as even those of the old Greeks, that of Plato, the Pythagoreans, and the early Stoics. In the first century, as Christianity was starting to grow and went out to conquer the world, there was absolutely no reason to think that driving the universal lifestyle of fornication from the world would take hold with any greater success than Plato's socialist ideals of civic moderation and justice, or the Pythagoreans' aims to improve moral character through procreations, or the early Stoics' plan to train citizens to achieve right reason and action through mutually friendly and communal sexual ideas. But Christianity conquered all! Fornication was banished to the house of whoredom and removed from cultured Christian society and since Christianity dominated, polite secular society also conformed to the Christian standards.

The Apostle Paul preaching in his missionary activities issued a universal and Christ-centered Biblical imperative against the fornicating lifestyles of the Greeks, Canaanites, and rebellious Israelites. Christian human sexual and reproductive concepts must be devoted strictly to the Biblical God through virginity, or paired marriage in the body of Christ. This pattern of sexual devotion provides the only permissible basis of social order, for all humanity, and as such must serve the Almighty God alone.

The Apostle Paul in the Christian Gospel insists that all those who become Christians must cease from dedicating any aspect of their minds or sexual bodies to their former pagan gods. Christians must vilify unbeliever pagan sexual heritage as wicked, and this heritage is even a deadly fornication against God Himself. Thus, a new order, a new order of virginity, celibacy, or marriage in the Lord, is the sole path to salvation and immortality. This, of course, was how God intended it from the beginning – one man and one woman, each woman to have her one, only, husband, and each man to have his one, only, wife.

Cathy's summary of fornication in Greek culture and her description of the Christian ministry of the Apostle Paul is very well written. She understands it very well.

Widespread Fornication in American Culture

Most grievously, massive widespread fornication is where the American culture is today. Americans are little different than the ancient Greeks, or the ancient rebellious Israelites who were little different from the Greeks. The nations surrounding the Israel homeland were known for their sexual corruption. Physical genital pleasure from fornication, adultery, sodomy, eroticism, etc. is now the norm of the day in America and Europe. The news and entertainment media is saturated with it. Fellowship with God is destroyed. Fornication is now the main fixation in American culture as it was in ancient Greek and Roman culture.

The nascent Church of Jesus Christ made war on the fornicating culture of Greeks, Romans, and rebellious Jews. The teaching of the Apostle Paul griped the Christian Church, so that as Christianity swept through the Roman Empire with its Greek culture roots, fornication was relegated to houses of prostitution. Endogamy marriage in the Lord within the Christian community became the norm in the Christian Church and in the general culture influenced by the Christian Church.

Through the ages is the continual battle between the forces of Satan seeking to corrupt man, and the influence of Christian teaching to guide man to fellowship with Almighty God and receive eternal life with Jesus. That is indeed the conflict. The conflict never goes away.

Dr. Gaca well understands the triumph of Christianity as it spread through the Roman Empire and put into practice the teachings of the Apostle Paul. Subsequently, the established Roman Catholic Church became the dominate political force among western Christian nations. Through the centuries this formal establishment Church made its own set of rules and created its own understandings about male and female relationships in which it placed a burden on its adherents, and also those who cooperated and wished not to be persecuted by the established political power structure. Those teachings and imperatives went beyond the teachings of the Apostle Paul.

Singleness of Some Believers

The Apostle Paul in the 7th chapter of Ist Corinthians wrote about the marriage relationship. He encouraged believers to remain single and not seek a spouse. Yet he said this was his opinion and not instruction from the Lord. Paul encouraged converts to remain as they were before they came to Jesus; if unmarried remain so, and if married to an unbeliever, remain married if the spouse consents to live with the believer.

The Roman Catholic Church and some other denominations have had a rule of celibacy for its priests, bishops, and popes. That Church policy is most likely based on the teachings of Paul. Also in the Church structure are convents for single women and monasteries for single men, not necessarily priests, where celibacy is practiced.

I have very little knowledge of such single person relationships in such churches, but it is understood that nuns are wed in some way to Christ Jesus. This is part of the same principle as taught by the Bible that the whole invisible Church of Jesus Christ is pictured as the bride of Jesus Christ. All believers in Jesus collectively are indeed pictured in the Bible as the bride of Christ.

Through understanding the Scriptures, I believe man is not complete unless a male and a female of man are united together in sexual union. That principle must indeed be modified for the man or woman who chooses to remain single for the glory of God. Singleness is certainly a very acceptable relationship. But as Paul advocates for the state of singleness, singleness is intended to cause a very special relationship to Jesus, and that the single person in a very special way, must then be devoted to the things of the Lord Jesus.

The Protestant Reformation changed some of the rules the Roman Catholic Church had imposed on its adherents. The reformers then established their own concepts of Christian marriage.

The Puritans left Europe for America and then established their own set of rules for the marriage relationship.

Americans for a couple of centuries considered Reformation Protestant understandings of marriage as the established acceptable norm.

I sincerely hope you, dear reader, have come to understand clearly God's mandate for the marriage relationship, as God through his apostles and prophets and Jesus the Godman Himself, teaches all of us through the words of the Bible.

THIRTEEN

Demise of American Culture

What is the conclusion of the matter? Where are we going? Man lives on planet earth. They eat, drink, work, make love, some get rich and so live off the productivity of others, some are slaves of others, and some slide down into the bonds of poverty and some remain trapped there.

Some like the Spaniards with military power acquire land from some original inhabitants who did steal it from previous indigenous people. Then a man, perhaps for example, one like Peralta who acquires the lands of what is now Oakland, California, settles down to a hopeful prosperous life only to have a swarm of American squatters, gold mining rejects, take his land from him. The squatters then lose the land, and it is turned over to greedy capitalists, who then plunder one another in quite an ongoing cycle.

Yes, a vast stage play, and it happens again and again, over and over throughout the world. In all of it; Almighty God rules.

Most of man sink into the oblivion of their sins and pass away, some in rest homes of squalor, some in hospitals for the rich, some (if they are lucky) from disease or accident that takes them away quick, or others in pain and suffering, or if luckier yet, in a fog of drug induced termination. All those of man die.

Some find the Lord Jesus and the love of God.

That is what it is all about. God is looking among man for those for eternal fellowship. Those selected from among man must hate evil. What better way to learn to hate evil then to be immersed in evil. Thus is human life on earth. Those who learn to hate evil, to utterly reject evil, can obtain the forgiveness of the evil they have done by coming to Jesus, and have their hearts - their inner essence - washed clean and purified.   Jesus said, "Think not that I came to save the righteous, but sinners." Those who never learn to hate evil, have tolerated evil in their lives, sink into the oblivion of their evil sins, and pass away.

Those who have come to exploit the relationship between God and man, by teaching a Satan inspired false religion to generate their own wealth and power and soft life in the kingdom of Satan, are taken by God and deposited into the fiery hot depth of hell, to suffer eternally for their terrible acts of blocking man from finding God and salvation. Yes, these, called stumbling blocks, have a very special place in the black hot fires of hell.

The Supreme Court of the United States of America legalized and forced same sex marriage as the force of law onto all the States. How is it that this marvelous nation has come to the point where nine old ugly hags and geezers decided deep moral issues? What audacity and presumption!   Thousands of years of civilization had finally produced an unwritten moral code where prosperity and peace could exist for the welfare of most of mankind living in the United States of America. This is to be thrown away because of radical filthy lucre corruption driven by propaganda of the media services? May God have mercy on the nation of the United States of America.

This same court ruled that the people of the State of Texas, which was an independent nation with its own laws before it joined the United States, cannot make a law prohibiting the practice of sodomy (6-3 vote - Rehnquist, Scalia, Thomas, dissenting), especially in a public display. One can only conclude the Supreme Court of the United States is a wicked corrupt institution.

Remember, stumbling blocks have a very special place in the black fires of hell. They will receive their just reward, and that includes the justices of the Supreme Court of the United States.

Only God the Father Knows the End

The gospel of Jesus Christ, the Son of God, has been preached throughout most of the earth. That is Jesus' requirement for the end of the age. Jesus says before the end, love will grow cold. It seems to be happening. Over the years false teachers have exploited Christians by predictions of the end of the earth for their own glory and lucre. Jesus said nobody knows the time of end, only God the Father knows. But Jesus said just as one can observe the clouds and know some weather is coming, so when you see the signs of the coming of the end, then the end will come.

Jesus said a time of unbelievable tribulation will occur before the end. Technology is now such that vast destructive powers are available to man. Few thought, except for some Ben Laden engineers, that a flight of a fuel laden commercial airliner could bring down a huge modern building edifice, the product of entrepreneurial capitalism.

What can come next? How about a multi-megaton nuclear device submerged in the bowels of an oil tanker seemingly wandering into the bay of Manhattan or San Francisco? Instead of the 3,000 people consumed in the twin tower event, maybe 30 million in a nuclear fireball? God rules, not man, and no matter how many security forces man uses to try to protect man, they will not be enough when the time comes for the great tribulation, and then the end.

If you are not yet a child of God, repent now before it is too late. Confess your sins and your inadequacy to handle life. Come to the feet of Jesus, worship Him, accept His love, and have your heart washed and purified with righteousness, receive the forgiveness of your sins through Jesus' shed blood, and have the Holy Spirit of God come to live within your spirit. Yes, be saved. You can then anticipate an eternity in fellowship with your loving God who made you.

Fornication Terribly Destructive

We have now come to modern America where the fornication culture as described by Gaca in the ancient world has come back to haunt modern America. Fornication is now the norm in American culture. So, where is America really now going?

Fornication is terribly destructive. Once fornication is accepted as normal, divorce is accepted as normal, and then follows sodomy, polygamy, bestiality, and others not even yet imagined by most of us, sexual corruption. Such corruption leads to a breakdown of cultural established norms. If such corruption is practiced, then why not practice thievery, lies, deception, and murder?

Eventually, such a culture must be ruled by a strong man, a dictator, who rewards his friends who do what he says, and destroys his enemies. The culture becomes little different from those of despots of old. Such despots create their own new enemies who then revolt and destroy the old established despot, and a cycle of war, revolt, and murder follow, one after another. Man returns to his barbaric roots and man lives like the Aztec tribes who made incessant war on one another. Then to intimidate their enemies, human sacrifice is initiated.

Is all that little different from radical Muslim extremists in 2015 operating in the Middle East? Performing deeds like those of the Aztecs, captives are murdered for the glory of their perceived Muslim god, and done in such a way that everybody on earth can witness it and be intimidated. Will this evil come and return to America? Will America become like that? It will, if Americans do not soon repent.

Yes, repentance must soon happen.

A great crime is even now being committed by the American national culture. The culture of fornication has produced a government sponsorship for the killing of little, innocent, nascent man children. This is murder. This is a terrible stench in God's nostrils. God is very, very patient. However, when the stench is too great, something will show up, perhaps something not unlike what happened when the Spaniards came to Mexico and devastated the place, but yes, through the Spaniards, an end was made to human sacrifice in Mexico.

It has now been a little over 40 years since abortion has been legalized by nine old geezers of man (7-2 vote - White and Rehnquist dissenting), corrupt men sitting in judgment on the highest court of the United States. 40 years is a Bible time of testing and trial. The people of the United States have had 40 years to rise up and put an end to this abomination, just as the Jews had 40 years to repent and weep over the One they pierced before their Temple was destroyed. The stench is becoming almost unbearable. Will the Spirit of God stir up someone or something to execute retribution and put an end to this terrible crime of murder?

Dictatorship Coming

One writer, recounting the history of Rome, said republics are reduced to democracies, and democracies are reduced to dictatorships. Such is exactly what happened to the Roman Empire. In all probability dictatorship is coming to the people of the United States. All of the wonderful freedoms enjoyed by its citizens, the remarkable entrepreneurial enterprise, the amazing inventions and technology, the widespread universal prosperity for almost everybody, the bread basket food production for all the world, all of this to be swallowed up into oblivion? We can only weep as we watch it happen.

God is not mocked.

Age of Delusion?

Are we entering an age of delusion? The sequence for the destruction of man, as men refuse to acknowledge God, is given in the 1st chapter of the book of Romans. The sequence ends up with depraved minds, the ultimate result of which is insanity. Is the American culture, therefore, entering a period of massive delusion and perhaps even massive insanity?

When my teen-age daughters (I have five of them) came to me and said they wanted to pierce their ears, in my primitive way I thought they were nuts and tried to discourage them. Their desire was to want to conform to the culture in which they were immersed and so make holes in their earlobes and hang something on them.

Why don't you put a bone through your nose like New Guinea aborigines do? But they would just laugh. They were under pressure exerted by their friends to do something, to be like everybody else. Even though the Old Testament scriptures indicate we are not to mark up or make holes in our bodies; I acquiesced.

It seemed like not a real big thing, so to discourage them and at the same time teach them something, they were told they must read a book called, *Extraordinary Popular Delusions*[13]. I hoped it would discourage them from making a habit of following the crowd. After much complaint and soft lovely female styles of manipulative speech making and pleading, it was usually reduced it to a chapter or two, but they almost never really studied it, and even if they did read it, they could not explain it. They just were not interested in concepts that involved deep thinking, were not interested in the understanding of historical follies and widespread human stupidity. They wanted to follow the crowd.

However, understanding massive delusions is very important. Delusions are terribly destructive and have in their execution an injection of insanity into the whole crowd swept up into the fun, excitement, and entertainment of the delusion.

Delusions that get collectively adopted by a large segment of a population have terrible, disastrous, consequences. Dictators and tyrants who want to control their country and then maybe the world, and lead where they want everybody to go, first use propaganda to form public opinion.

A good example of this is Adolf Hitler and his Nazi Party. Then as a group coalesces, perhaps even a minority, around the party line as established by propaganda, the perpetrators silence their opposition by intimidation, perhaps even killing some of those who oppose them. Then they like the Nazis consolidate their power and go on to commit great heinous crimes, such as the Nazi slaughter of about six million innocent Jews, and engage in a very destructive horrible aggressive world war in which millions were killed.

Through my companies I was for 16 years a Registered Commodity Futures Trading Advisor, managing speculation money for brokerage firm clients. Little mini delusions are what drive financial bubbles. These bubbles of delusion can make a nimble trader very, very rich quickly.

In past money management days, speculation clients were given a copy of the Mackay book on delusions. I studied the book carefully and applied technical mathematical principals to exploit and take advantage of mini delusions; so I understand a little of human mass delusions.

The homosexual/fornication campaign to destroy the man/woman marriage relationship, the rise of the homosexual agenda, transsexualism, etc., etc., in American culture, against all rational analysis and understanding of human history, is just such a Satanic driven mass delusion. It too is driven by propaganda.

The modern machine like vast politicized fornication/homosexual movement is just such a delusion even as that practiced by the Nazis. Opposition is silenced by intimidation. Even parents, who have lived out a good portion of their lives in prosperity and contentment in the fantastic opportunity culture of the United States, find their children returning home from college, moving in with them, and teaching them the new sexual ideas adopted through propaganda driven by the self-appointed elites in colleges. The parents then change their ideas and conform to the new propaganda line not wishing to be seen as old fuddy-duddies.

The main stream media and the vast network of the mass communication processes of the United States, is now largely driven by propaganda. People who see evil of it and protest get quite intimidated. The whole is a vast propaganda fraud.

Thousands of years of civilization have shown the proper moral direction society is to take. Is all that now going to be changed and thrown away? No, it cannot be. It is against all the unwritten laws which govern healthy productive society. Indeed, the vast evil of the campaign will eventually be revealed. However, America through the process will suffer terrible evil consequences. Through the abandonment of solid moral cultural norms, evil comes.

Consider an example from the Bible. The Prophet Habakkuk places a plea before God that the men of his culture are doing evil. The Prophet complains to God, and tells God He ought to do something about it. God responds and says to the Prophet, just wait, the Chaldeans are coming.

The Prophet shouts, "No, no, no, not those people. They are very wicked, bad, ugly people who kill and murder and destroy in a horrible, horrible way. Not them Lord!" Well, the rest is history and the Israelite nation was destroyed by the Chaldeans. The lesson from this is we must be careful what we pray for.

Eventuality, a massive fraud delusion campaign driven by propaganda gets discovered, gradually, by more and more people. Then the whole thing collapses. Mackey's book has provided good examples of mass delusion and the evil consequences. The great paper money prosperity bubble created by John Law for the French, and the terrible financial collapse of the French nation that followed, substantially contributed in the next generation to the cause of the French Revolution and then the rise of the dictator, Napoleon. Napoleon radically changed cultural norms and became the scourge of Europe and caused the slaughter of millions. Eventually the British and Prussians defeated his army. Then the British, in secret, did a very un-British thing - they poisoned him. But that was the just and fitting end for Napoleon.

Mackay described several examples of massive delusions such as widespread alchemy projects (turning lead into gold) funded by many rich nobles and nations, the Crusades, witch mania, haunted houses, follies of great cities, admiration of thieves, and relics. Of course, the great financial delusion events like the Dutch Tulipomania, the South-Sea Bubble, and the Mississippi Scheme are well covered and well worth a great read to understand massive delusions of history.

One of the crusades for the taking of Palestine from the Muslims was called the Children's Crusade. Two charismatic monks went around Europe and proclaimed it is God's will that the children go to Palestine and chase the Muslims Infidels out! About 30,000 teen age children marched out of Europe for Palestine, some to die in ship wrecks, some to be just slaughtered, and some to be made into slaves for the Muslims. The girls were made into sex toys, and the boys were emasculated and made into Janissaries --- eunuchs who fight the Muslim wars. What terrible evil folly! But it shows what propaganda can do.

An almost unbelievable delusion, which when it was occurring was very real, and was on a march to rule the world, was the Lenin/Stalin Bolshevik Communism that created the Soviet Union. As one looks back on it, it seems to have been impossible. Was the great historical nation of Russia taken over by a few radical revolutionaries? In hindsight, it seems incredible. But it happened and the Soviets ruled for 70 years. The whole thing was built on propaganda and a secret police force to intimidate and silence opposition. But the Soviets came near to ruling the world.

I have characterized myself as a warrior in the American cold war with the Soviets. I was not a leader but a grunt laboring at developing electronic radar devices, and developing force level planning tools for the military of the United States. I saw long before hand the beginning of the end of communism as practiced in the Soviet Union. The Soviets could not keep up in technology development. In the 1970's United States' missiles, because of integrated circuit navigation innovations, could directly hit and go right down the Soviet missile silo holes. The Soviets did not have that capability and would not have it for a long time.

Then the coming end of the Soviets was confirmed in my mind when I saw a cartoon. It was a drawing of a man looking down into the subways of Moscow and telling the Russian crowd way down in the catacombs, "It's ok now, you can come out. President Reagan said he was only kidding." Yes, the communist intimidators had lost. Reagan rattling the saber sent Muscovites into hiding. Very funny, but it thoroughly exposed the Soviet ruling elites as a fraud.

There is another massive fraud going on right now in California as of circa 2015. A politically created water shortage is providing the ruling elites the opportunity to expand their political control over that magnificent state. California is an extremely bountiful place. The wonderful Sierra Nevada Mountains trap moisture from winter storm systems and turn it into snow so the water in the form of snow is stored and released slowly down rivers to reservoirs and to underground storage in the San Joaquin and Sacramento valley aquifers; they are huge.

There is a vast Pacific Ocean with water extending thousands of miles to the west. Quite lacking is the political vision to store water and make fresh water from salt water. The technology is there; it can be done, but propaganda driven by elites who really should be called communists, as they think like communists, they act like communists, but call themselves progressive or other nice sounding names, halt any logical environmentally sound development. California innocents are paying a terrible price just so the elites can enjoy their nice philosophical prerogatives. Again, eventually, this fraud will be discovered. Those elites should be fearful as this fraud could very well produce a lot of real anger.

So, given all those examples of delusions, where is America going? The male/female monogamy marriage relationship has been around since the beginning of the human race. It is the foundation of successful human civilization. Will all inherited marriage structure of successful society be changed and thrown away contrary to the coding program of DNA within humans which drives and determines style and manifestation of human existence? To try to arbitrarily change that for something different, something some people would like it to be, rather than what it really is, as if they were God, is a delusion. But it is a delusion, the implementation of which will cause great evil, mass suffering, death, and vast corruption of multitudes of people.

Unfortunately, from massive delusions it takes a long time to recover. Men love lies. Men love delusions. According to Desiderius Erasmus[14] writing in the early 1500's, "Folly makes society delightful." Yes, men have not changed in 500 years - only their fears of who might hang them for blasphemy. In the end truth always, without fail, wins. But the price for folly and delusion, to be paid in misery and suffering, is huge. Put this principal into your mind: Delusions, driven by fraud, cause great evil. Remember, God's solution for evil is more evil.

In 2015, the Supreme Court of the United States ruled (5-4 vote - Alito, Roberts, Scalia, Thomas, dissenting) that all the states of the United States must issue marriage licenses for the marriage of men with men and women with women. What unbelievable presumption! What folly! What delusion! What evil!

If the Court can issue such rulings it can also issue rules to behead men and women for blasphemy! Will that be long in coming? Nothing is impossible. All it takes is a determined minority and a passive citizenry wanting peace and quiet in their own time, willing to let the radicals have what they think they want, even though it is very stupid, very foolish, very destructive, and very evil.

Beheading has been going on in areas of the world where Muslim extremists rule. A few decades ago almost all of us Americans could not even have imagined such a thing. Yes, evil begets evil; therefore, vast evil is coming to the United States of America. You think that is impossible? Where is the republican form of government or even democracy when five Supreme Court judges, in fact, five old hags and geezers, make up law out of whole cloth and dictate to the citizens of the United States a corruption of all the moral standards proven by history? Then all the governors of the several states and their legislatures do nothing, and the political opposition party does nothing, and plays like it is dead? Yes, evil, vast evil is coming to the people of the United States.

However, let us end this long dissertation on a happy note. Eventually, this delusion like all delusions will run its course. When will the present great massive fornication/homosexual delusion get revealed, get discovered by a large segment of the American people? Who knows? It will eventually be discovered. You can do your part to help in discovery.

As an example of a small individual effort against evil driven government, consider the French nobleman, knowing the collapse of the Mississippi scheme of John Law would come, converted all of his John Law paper money into gold. Because the scheme perpetrators had made it a crime to own gold, he hid his gold in the bottom of a huge wagon of bull and cow manure, put on peasant clothes, saturated himself in manure, and drove the wagon over the border out of France. He financially survived but most of the French landed gentry did not.

So you, too, do your part. Speak in any assembly, around friends, among associates, in your church, organized group, anywhere, and everywhere in your community. Oppose and speak out against any and all homosexual propaganda and especially that promoted in the public school system.

Speak out strongly against teaching children the homosexual life style. Expose the propaganda as a fraud to as many people as you can. Do not fear the opposition. They are frauds, and deep down in their hearts the frauds know they are frauds. Their sin and corruption will slowly destroy their lives and lead them in the direction of misery and insanity.

Yes: Again, what should you do? Watch for opportunity. Keep your cool and worship Jesus. Trust the pure Holy Spirit of God within you to lead you in the way you ought to go. It may not be pleasant and you may even become a martyr. You may even lose your head on the chopping block.

Remember there is a special place in the Heavens of the Eternities for those who are martyrs for the cause of The Lord Jesus Christ. Although nobody wants to be killed, to lose your life as a testimony of your faith in the Lord Jesus Christ, your God and your Savior, would be a very glorious eternal ending of your life on earth!

In the mean time, consider how Christ rules his kingdom in the following chapters.

FOURTEEN

Physical Creation Space-Time

"In the beginning was the Word, and the Word was with God, and the Word was God. He was in the beginning with God. All things came into being through Him, and apart from Him nothing came into being that has come into being. In Him was life, and the life was the Light of men. The Light shines in the darkness, and the darkness did not comprehend it." John 1:1-5

The Westminster Confession, the last of the great reformation declarations, proclaims two sources of truth --- creation and the Bible. God did the creation through the Word. The Apostle, John, quoted above, provides an extremely terse, very brief, description of the beginning of everything. The Word did it. That Word, John proclaims, is the man, Jesus Christ.

Recent discoveries of the substance of the creation, or let's call it the universe, have provided for modern man substantial additional information for the understanding of God, of the substance of God, through observation of the universe.

One purpose of this writing is to give understanding of the relationship between God's omnipotent rule and that which causes things to happen, that is, does God cause additional things to happen based on what has happened?

So how is it that, The Man, Jesus Christ, who lived as a man on the earth from about four BC to about thirty AD, creates the universe and everything within it? Yes indeed, a very, very profound claim. To try to understand, examine a little of the nature of the universe.

Sovereignty of God

The sovereignty of God, that God rules over and maintains His creation, is a concept emphasized in many places in the Bible. Yet man, obviously, has free will, yet limited by time and space. These two concepts, to use the old word from High School geometry, are in-congruent. Meaning, in our limited human experience, both cannot be true at the same time, yet they must both be true if we are to believe the Bible. Christian understanding is that both concepts are true.

Now let me add a third to the conundrum. Since God dwells outside as well as inside time and space, that which He also created, God is not subject to his own creation so God can act and does act from outside of time and space, as well as inside of time and space.

Therefore, in Gods realm of dwelling, in infinitude, there is no causality! Meaning that nothing causes anything else in what is essentially God's infinite domain of everything!

This is because the concept of causality requires action in the sequence of time passing. First an event occurs, and later another event occurs, the second event caused by the action result of the first event.

That is essentially the definitions of causality. Time does not exist or pass by in the dwelling existence of God. God is timeless. God created time.

This writing attempts to deal with these concepts. It is desired to understand a little more about the God who made us and loves us and as the Bible teaches, wants to have sweet lovely fellowship with us, humans, who are of man, just as the Creator, Jesus Christ, is of man, and therefore, is a man --- a man who is God in the flesh of a man.

Truth

The Roman procurator, Pilot, when he was about to issue a judicial judgment and condemn, The Man Jesus Christ, to His death by crucifixion, said to Jesus, "What is truth?"

Yes, what is truth? There are three sources of truth. The Bible says examine creation itself for truth. That is the first source. The second is correct thinking and understanding derived from logical processes. The third is direct revelation from God.

Direct revelation from God is given by prophets and apostles. The Bible defines several requirements for a valid prophet. The prophet must be a Hebrew, and he or she must never be wrong. This rules out almost all people who claim direct revelation from God. The word of God, the Bible, is composed of writings of apostles and prophets

So we must understand the Bible, examine creation, and use correct understanding and analysis to establish truth.

Relativity

A theory with very substantial proof by observation and measurement, called the theory of relativity, was first proposed by that great scientific hero, Albert Einstein. Great scientific discoveries are made when an observation in the real physical world is made and the scientist asks himself, why is this true, and what are the consequences of this observed truthful fact?

In Einstein's day an observation was made that was very counter intuitive and seemed to go against all the understandings of physics up to that day. The observation, called the Michelson/Morley experiment showed that the speed of light in space was the same in any reference frame. Wow, what does this mean? A reference frame is essentially how does one look at things and measure things from any place in space in comparison to looking at things from any other place. The fact that light travels at the same velocity in any reference frame anywhere leads to the special theory of relativity.

Relativity theory has some very interesting non-intuitive surprising consequences. The mass of an object as it is approached is a function of the relative velocity between the observer and the object. The mass gets greater and greater as the speed between the object and the observer approach the speed of light. In addition the space between the object and the observer gets smaller and smaller, and the measurement of time between the object and the observer gets smaller and smaller. This is just astounding! It is very counter intuitive. Our intuitions as earth dwellers told us that time and space are fixed and are the same yesterday, today, and tomorrow. Relativity is very hard to believe.

Equivalence of Gravitational Mass and Inertial Mass

Then there is a second theory of Einstein called general relativity. Einstein used the already known observation of the fact that the inertial mass of an object is the same as the gravitational mass. Inertial mass is that resistance to motion when a force is applied to a mass object to make it move. Gravitational mass is the force exerted on an object by the presence of another mass such as the earth. Einstein had the insight to understand that inertial mass operations and forces must then be identical to gravitational operations and forces. Again, this is something very astounding and would not be perceived from intuitive insight.

From this understanding came Einstein's general theory of relativity. This very well established theory presents time and space as dilated by the presence of mass. As one approaches the earth, for example, space itself contracts and time slows down. However, time and space are intrinsically related through the never changing velocity of light (true in a dielectric free medium), and the combination is called four dimensional space-time. Space-time contracts as a mass body is approached, just as space-time contracts when one descends in a gravitational field. The effects are the same and are equivalent.

These two theories tell us much about creation, about the nature of the universe, and since God through Jesus Christ created the Universe out of nothing, these very well substantiated theories tell us a little about God.

Essentially, time and space are not absolute ways to look at things. As we humans dwell on the earth we are enveloped in time and space.   We are confined to the earth with the exception of a few astronauts.

All of our thinking and dwelling is in the space of the earth and time on the earth as it passes by. Thus we think time and space are everything. No, this is false. The observation of the universe of creation tells us time and space are both variable, and fixed space-time is not the essential thing for our existence.

This physics of creation tells us the relativity of space-time is reality and ultimately is the main thing of our existence. As a consequence of all this, correct observational requirements of the universe, depend on the observer's state of being and the local space-time from which the observer observes.

From the understanding of this equivalence of inertial mass and gravitational mass, Einstein developed a mathematical equation, called a differential equation, which described this essence in mathematical terms of the relativity theory behind these observations. Differential equations are part of the mathematical subject called calculus. Calculus and the differential equations of calculus to some people are a tough mathematical college course that is often used to separate the men and women from the boys and girls at the beginning of scientific studies.

There are multiple solutions to differential equations. The inverse of differential calculus is integral calculus. So in order to obtain the solution to a differential equation one needs to perform integrations. Derivatives of constants are zero, so the solution to a differential equation can have any value for constants that might have appeared in the solution to the equation before a differential operation is performed.

Einstein understood that solutions to the differential equation that described the universe gave an expanding universe. Since all men are corrupt and come short of the Glory of God, as stated by the Westminster Confession of Faith, and Einstein is no exception, Einstein chose for constants of integration ones that simply compensated to a great extent for universe expansion and so provided a steady state universe without expansion.

He did this because he wanted the scientific community to readily accept his theoretical results, as most physicists in those days believed in a steady state universe. Steady state means the universe is not expanding or contracting and things of the overall universe are as they always have been and will continue in the same vein. Years later he admitted this was a great error as in fact the universe had been found to be expanding, and this expansion of space has been now found, in this our own time, to be accelerating.

In Einstein's day many physicists did not want to believe that some god was involved in creation of the universe. An expanding universe implied that the universe had a beginning. A beginning implied an agent of creation, and that agent had to be some kind of god. Therefore, a steady state universe without expansion was a much more acceptable theory to the physics establishment of Einstein's day.

Now days we understand the universe had a beginning of time, and of space, and of matter, and of energy, and space is expanding. Now because the constant c, also the speed of light in a dielectric free vacuum, relates space to time, so that time and space are intrinsically related, and form a four dimensional relationship, time must also expand with space! We call this space-time expansion. Astounding!

What does this mean? Is our sense of time passing only the expansion of what we call time? That I will leave to some young intelligent experimental physicist to prove. But in this writing assume that to be true and explore the consequences of time and space expanding or contracting together, in what is all the same togetherness, in the reality of the space-time of the universe.

Space Stretching

There are many passages in the Bible that say that space is being stretched out. I am quite attentive to these expressions. Surely the translators could have found other expressions to convey the idea that the heavens were made by God. But many expressions occur in the Bible that convey the concept that God is stretching out the heavens, meaning that space itself is being expanded or stretched.

Following are verses from the Bible discussing the stretching of the heavens.

"Do you not know? Have you not heard? Has it not been declared to you from the beginning? Have you not understood from the foundations of the earth? It is He who sits above the circle of the earth, and its inhabitants are like grasshoppers, who stretches out the heavens like a curtain and spreads them out like a tent to dwell in." Isaiah 40:22

"Thus says the God the Lord, who created the heavens and stretched them out, who spread out the earth and its offspring, who gives breath to the people on it and spirit to those who walk in it." Isaiah 42:5

"Thus says the Lord, your Redeemer and the one who formed you from the womb, I, the Lord am the maker of all things, stretching out the heavens by Myself, and spreading out the earth all alone." Isaiah 44:24

"It is I who made the earth, and created man upon it. I stretching out the heavens with My hands. And I ordained all their host." Isaiah 45:12

"Surely My hand founded the earth, and My right hand spread out the heavens, when I call to them they stand together." Isaiah 48:13

"That you have forgotten the Lord your Maker, who stretched out the heavens and laid the foundations of the earth." Isaiah 51:13

"Bless the Lord, O my soul! O Lord my God, You are very great; covering Yourself with light as with a cloak, stretching out the heavens like a tent curtain." Psalm 104:2

"He stretches out the north over empty space, and hangs the earth on nothing." Job 26:7

"It is He who made the earth by his power, Who established the world by His wisdom, and by understanding He has stretched out the heavens." Jeremiah 10:12

"It is He who made the earth by his power, Who established the world by his wisdom. And by his understanding He stretched out the heavens." Jeremiah 51:15

"The burden of the Lord concerning Israel: Thus declares the Lord who stretches out the heavens, lays the foundations of the earth, and forms the spirit of man within him." Zechariah 12:1

These verses clearly establish that the Bible teaches that God stretched out the heavens. Many other words could have been used to establish that God created the heavens. Why is the word translated as stretch used? Clearly God, through the Spirit of God, wants us to understand that God stretches out the heavens or in modern understanding of the physics and descriptive words about the universe, God stretches out space-time, since one element of space-time cannot expand without the other element expanding.

FIFTHTEEN

Quantum Physics

There is a very profound set of concepts that govern and control the universe. Quantum physics rules over everything. Quantum physics is mysterious and is very counter intuitive, yet has been proven true. Quantum physics principles are used all the time by scientists and engineers to design and build all the marvelous devices we use every day. Quantum physics rules in chemical reactions and molecular structures of all the drugs and other stuff we use to make all the astounding things for our lives.

Basic theory of quantum physics reduces everything to what are called wave functions[15]. Wave functions are a sort of mystical mathematical expression. When a physical measurement is made or a reaction occurs, as in chemical reaction, when it happens, the wave functions collapse into statistics and probability distributions describing the event. As a preposterous example, consider the composite wave function of all of your body. There is a finite probability, infinitely small, that right now your body is on the moon.

For that to happen you would have to normally wait an almost infinitely long time. But yet there is an extremely small probability for that to be your state. This raises all kinds of very interesting possibilities. But these quantum physics principles govern the universe in which you live, and govern everything you enjoy using!

Evidence: Man without Excuse

The Bible says in the first chapter of Romans that God has put enough information and evidence in creation so that man is without excuse. An understanding of Creation gives one a little insight and understanding about God.

It turns out in the quantum physics of understanding of the universe, everything of the mass matter of the universe through its creation, is the result of these statistical amplitudes derived from the wave functions. All is the result of what seems like the product of statistical distributions and randomness and averages of randomness and integrations over randomness. The whole of the mass of the universe is represented by wave functions.

So, conclude that God integrates over the randomness and statistical distributions and makes everything happen moment by moment. The movement is from history of the past to the unknown future. The Bible says God knows the result of every roll of the dice before they are rolled, so God knows every result of integration over randomness and distributions, and so God maintains the Universe. The Bible teaches that not one hair will fall from a head of man without the will of God.

Schrodinger's Cat

One concept of quantum physics that young physicists are cautioned not to think about deeply, as it may lead to quandaries that potentially might ruin young physicist's minds, was presented by a past hero of quantum physics, Erwin Schrodinger. Schrodinger came up with the wave function mathematical equation which provides solutions to quantum physics problems. This equation is very basic and is used by engineers and scientists to solve quantum physics problems.

Schrodinger dreamed up some thinking to ridicule and refute strange understanding of quantum physics. It is a mind/thought experiment called Schrodinger's Cat[16]. Most everybody laughed and went on with scientific inquiry and stopped thinking about the ramifications of strange, seemingly ridiculous principles of quantum physics.

But about forty years later, experiments[17] by Freedman and Clauser were performed at the University of California that proved what was called the Copenhagen explanation of Schrodinger's Cat to be true.

Schrodinger imagined a box where a Cat is placed along with a radioactive source and a poison that kills the Cat when the radioactive substance emits radiation. So the Cat is either alive or dead depending on the emission of radiation. But according to quantum physics the Cat is both alive and dead at the same time. When the Box is opened, the event of discovery of the Cat reduces to a probably distribution as to whether the Cat is alive or dead. Yes indeed, very strange.

Understand the wave function of the Cat extends over the whole universe. So no matter what kind of box the cat is placed, or where it is placed, even if a quadrillion miles away, when the cat is discovered the event of the cat's death reduces to a probability distribution. The result of this Copenhagen understanding indicates the wave function, for example, of a particle like an electron or proton, therefore, extends over the whole universe and does not follow or be subject to the rules of relativity physics.

When a measurement is made or an observation is made on a particle's wave function, the wave function collapses into a probability distribution. So when you do something like using a sort of amp meter to detect an electron, the electron's wave function collapses into the probability that the electron has just passed through your amp meter.

As another preposterous example, to give a sort of picture of the concept, assume for a moment that your body's composite wave function extends over the whole universe, which it does, and then when you observe yourself in a mirror, the composite wave function collapses into a probability that you are most likely to be in the space-time spot where you are now located looking at yourself.

This may seem like an absurd example of the concept, but it is essentially true. Quantum physics almost takes on an intrinsic spiritually. Some physicists have suggested that. Now this is not some speculation. In July of 2017, reports of Chinese experiments confirmed action at a distance (to a space satellite and back) observation proving again the Copenhagen understanding. This is how the universe operates. These principles and the equations of quantum physics are used to make things. Things you enjoy using --- things that are real. Lots of physicists would like to create a new theory of quantum physics and change these understandings. Many have worked on it now for almost 100 years, and no good new theory has been developed, and so it has not happened. So we are stuck with modern quantum physics. These principals are not going to change. This is what God made!

The purpose of this writing is to give you some understanding. These concepts of relativity and quantum physics tell us things about the universe of God's creation so you can understand a little about God. Now perhaps, so there may occur less doubt in your mind about the awesome power of God, God's omnipotence, God's infinite presence anywhere and everywhere in His creation, God governing His creation, understand that God is continuously making everything happen in His creation.

After all, if the wave function of an electron extends over the whole universe, certainty God extends over the whole universe, since He made it. Yes, the wave functions of everything extend over the whole universe. And then, astoundingly, the wave functions of the composite you, extend over the whole universe too.

Free Will

Within these wave functions is free will. This is demonstrated by the Schrodinger's Cat thinking experiment, as within the box of observation, a radioactive atom just like the Cat, decides by itself when it is to pass on or decay into something else. One cannot predict when an individual radioactive atom is to decay. There is only a distribution of possibilities within the observed known statistics, which God drives, of when an atom might decay. Identical particles with identical wave functions, identical in every possible way, do not behave identically.

This is the physics of the universe which God made. Unpredictability of things happens all the time. So you too, like the cat in Schrodinger's Cat Box, through the integrated composite wave function that is you, have free will.

SIXTEEN

Free Will, Basic You, NOW

So God has given you the opportunity to make free will choices. Your life here on earth is a tremendous opportunity to learn to make good choices. Making good and bad choices is what life is all about. We are spiritual beings. We have a sense of eternity in our inner being, our hearts. We are constantly making the free will decisions of life.

Is your life like what God said of the people on the earth before He destroyed them with a flood of water --- that the thinking of the heart of man is only evil continually?

Yes, believe it, we of man are corrupt. We have a corrupt nature, and according to God Himself, the thoughts of our man hearts are only evil continually. However, there is the most wonderful possibility that one has come to believe in Truth, the Truth of Jesus Christ.

Ramifications of Free Will

Now consider the ramifications of free will and think again about the mind experiment of Schrodinger's Cat. The atomic particle in the box in essence decides by itself when it is to decay into other particles. When the box is opened, the Cat determines itself to be either alive or dead --- the event caused by an observer looking into the box. Is this not the Cat's free will?

Again, understand, identical nuclear particles, identical in every possible way, do not behave identically. Particles decay in the time of the particles own choosing creating a statistical distribution of decay events in time.

So quantum physics which governs the universe, and is very well established experimentally, has built in free will. This is the reality of the universe. Anything can decide for itself when it is to transform itself into something else by the rules of quantum physics of God's stupendous, marvelous, creation.

By extension of this very microscopic observable physical truth, your body composed of many particles, too has the capability to decide what to do in any situation, subject to the rules of quantum physics and space-time relativity. Now humans have brains to make decisions. Particles do not have brains; so think of particle free will as an anthropomorphic analogy.

So yes, you have free will, but God determines the consequences and the outcome!

Free Will Consequences

Decisions of free will have consequences. If I like Cain, rise up and kill my brother, did God or some other spiritual being make me do it? NO, NO, NO! I am responsible. I did it. I made a free will decision to do it. So the vast evil and corruption that drives much human society and civilization, is the result of countless of man making their own free will decisions, which foster evil and create vast ugliness in human civilization.

Yes, mankind is depraved and incapable of doing real good, as the Westminster Confession of Faith and Catechism proclaims.

Sin and evil are contrary to God's nature, contrary to His basic being. It has often been said that God hates sin. I have not found a really good reference in the Bible that clearly makes that statement. However, from the Book of Romans the Apostle Paul writes, "For the wrath of God is revealed from heaven against all ungodliness and unrighteousness". (Romans 1:18) And, "There is none righteous, not even one; there is none who understands, there is none who seeks for God; all have turned aside, together they have become useless". (Romans 3:10-11) And God has given the Law, which commands us not to do certain acts such as the act of murder of Cain's brother, Able.

However, Able was murdered before God gave man the law. Yet God severely punished Cain.

So God has put the understanding of the evil in doing murder in man's inner being, the heart of man, and so made them responsible for the consequences. The Bible says that sin will be punished; by death here and now, and then the second death in eternity. This is the consequence of sin and evil. Sin is very destructive and has terrible, terrible, consequences. So God has put the consciousness of evil in the most inner being of each man person and then made them responsible for knowing and doing evil.

The Apostle Paul in the Book of Romans, Chapters six and seven, teaches there are three categories of sin for people who might call themselves Christian. First is sin as a lifestyle. If you have sin as a lifestyle you are simply not a Christian, and you are doomed to hell, the place of the dead. You are a slave of sin and your life belongs to that evil spiritual being called Satan or the Devil. He seeks your demise and destruction. He is the father of lies and deception.

The second category of sin is man choosing to sin once in a while. Yes, you know what is right and wrong; you know what sin is deep within your being, and yet you choose to do the sin. This choosing to sin has roughly three consequences. First, you become a slave to sin. Sin becomes your master. It rules over you and you become ruled by it. Second, you begin to loathe yourself. You become disgusted with yourself and begin to hate yourself. You are ashamed of yourself. You become spiritually unstable and confused, doubting the very existence of God. Third, sin leads to death. You start to die here and now. Your whole being starts to act like it is dead. Wonderful things that used to move your being and cause you to enjoy life seem common and unenjoyable. You choose reckless sources to obtain contentment for your soul, so you seek possession of things; you seek diversions that take away the feeling of dying, and so you do drugs and become addicted. Death eventually spreads throughout your whole existence.

Paul's third category of sin is inadvertent sin. Your body does what your soul does not want it to do. You are not practicing what you want to do, but are doing the things you hate. You agree with the Laws of God, confessing that God's rules for living are good, but do the very things you wish not to do. So Paul concludes you are not then the one doing the sin but the sinful nature within you. You see a different law in the members of your body waging war with the law of your mind making you a prisoner of the law of sin in your body members.

Paul asks the very profound question, who will deliver me and you from this body of death? It is Jesus Christ! Jesus has set you, the Christian, free, and there is no condemnation. You have been joined to your Savior, Jesus Christ.

Christ the Answer

So Christians have this fantastically great unfathomable hope. Jesus Christ, God in the flesh of a man, came to earth and has paid the price God demands of all the sin of mistakes, errors, crimes, and trespasses, and the sin of the basic nature of man received from forebears. Christ has cleansed, or given Christian, a new clean heart, washed by the blood of Jesus Christ Himself. God sees the clean heart, and that heart becomes a wonderful fragrance to God, and so God loves that clean heart person you are as a Christian.

Life in the world-realms of the flesh, soul, and spirit, is a struggle and full of trials and trouble, but with the love of God and a clean pure heart, you can go forth with confidence and get prepared for full awesome life in eternity.

Body Wave Function

So now let us go back to a little physics to gain additional understanding. If the composite wave function of your body (that is you) extends over the whole universe of creation, then miracles can happen to your body with no additional effort by God, as a lot of what are called miracles, are just possible events in the distribution of possibilities. The prayers and pleas of your mind are immediately in God's presence, and God can select the point in any distribution of possibilities to answer your needs and requests.

Now we Christians already know this by faith, because we believe God, and have experienced God working in our lives. We believe all that God speaks to us. But now, here in this our own time, physical science has discovered in these last days, that yes, the quantum physics of the universe indicates anything can happen subject to the probability rules of that happening. Because God controls the outcome of each roll of the dice, God controls the outcome of every statistical event thing that happens! Marvelous! Praise God! God is sovereign! Praise you Jesus Christ, we worship You!

Basic You

So what is this basic you that makes free will decisions? In the first chapter it was established that Jesus Christ, in a pre-incarnated manifestation is demonstrated by analogy, through a fuzzy pictured representation to be structured as a human man, as indicated by the Tabernacle of the Hebrews. (Exodus Chapters 25-27) This fuzzy pictured thing indicated four areas of the tabernacle to be representations, by analogy, of four world-realms. Since Jesus Christ is of man and we humans are of man, we also exist in four world-realms as Jesus Christ as a man did and does.

To review a little for your understanding, these four world-realms are first, the body of flesh in space-time physical creation; let's call it the physical world-realm. The second is the world-realm of souls, with the thinking and planning of the minds, wills, and emotions. Let's call it, and define it, as the soul world-realm. The third is the spiritual world-realm. The fourth world-realm is the essential you, deep within your spirit, in the Bible it is called heart. From the heart come the deep motivations of life --- the sense of right and wrong come out of the heart.

In review then, most of mankind are consumed and motivated by the body in the first world-realm --- by the needs and desires of the human physical body. Their minds constantly focus on satisfying body wants and needs, and so they mainly dwell in the world-realm of the flesh. In their lives wants and needs of the flesh drive the thinking of the soul.

Others, usually the more affluent of mankind, are driven by the thinking of their minds, intellectual pursuits and dreams, and the ramifications and opportunities of civilization, which occur in this second world-realm, that of souls. The soul world-realm is a vast thing of design and conception of sundry activities, intellectual pursuits, and projects of civilization.

The Bible says the design and operational procedures of the vast universe in which we all live were all conceived in the mind of Christ. So Christ is responsible for space-time, relativity, and quantum physics. Christ designed the whole thing so we Christians of human mankind would come to know and love Him.

Within man spirit is the basic underlying thing that drives righteous honest man --- the empathy for others, the sense of right and wrong, and the respect and love for other humans. All these qualities are motivated by spirit within the spirit world-realm.

Deep within the man spirit is the quintessential essence of man, the heart. The Bible says that when a man becomes a Christian, Christian is given a new clean heart, or as some scriptures say, a washed purified heart. Out of the heart come the essential motivations and direction of life.

Free will is exercised and initiated through the heart. The Bible says the unwashed heart of the depraved devise evil continuously.

NOW

Decisions of life come out of man's heart, but these decisions are executed in the real physical world-realm in what one brilliant experimental physicist, Richard Muller[18], Professor of Physics at the University of California, has called NOW.

Some theoretical physicists have postulated, in what is called String Theory, that the universe is constituted in a minimum of eleven dimensions. They postulate that the presently observed three space dimensions have associated with each space dimension, two additional highly curved up space dimensions. So these nine space dimensions plus forward time and backward time give eleven.

So postulate an additional time dimension using Muller's term NOW, giving us a minimum of twelve dimensions. I suggest we understand all of time by postulating three time dimensions --- forward time, backward time, and NOW.

I suggest what has happened in the past of time is just history and cannot be changed, and therefore, has no influence on time or the future of time in itself. Everything that has ever happened is just received and recorded into history as a past event, and has passed into what has been, and in no way is ever to be influenced or changed by any event in time again.

Separate all the past, all that has been, from the active activity of what will happen. Postulate that NOW is the crucial thing and once NOW has happened, what has happened will pass into history. The past is that which already has happened and has been in some cases recorded by man.

Of course, we Christians understand that God has recorded everything that has ever happened in vast books for the final judgment. (Revelation 20:11-12) Many of man used to think that was impossible, but now we learn the National Security Agency of the United States of America, has recorded in computer storage arrays, every stroke of every keyboard of every computer and communication thing that is connected to the internet. God can do anything and He is much better at it than man.

This concept of NOW, as being the source of what will possibly happen in the future, is contrary to what was believed up to a few years ago when philosophers, even Christian leaders, science and mathematics experts, and a lot of physicists, taught everything was pre-determined --- that the future is laid out continuing from what was in or what was happening from the past. They taught the future was derived from the past as time continued on following the deterministic rules of science and mathematics.

Modern quantum physics through its principals of uncertainty and statistical choice has now completely overturned this determinism theory. Most past theories have, therefore, been proved to be false.

Thus postulate there is backward time, forward time, and NOW. The future is the extension of NOW and is unknown. NOW is what is happening at the moment and can be influenced or changed by free will of mankind.

Muller suggested that the expansion of space-time of the universe provides us with our sense of NOW. When I first came to understand from direct reports of scientific observation of the universe, that the universe was expanding, and that the expansion is accelerating, I understood that time must also be expanding.

I was excited to discover the writings of Muller, and understood that Muller was thinking along the same lines and conceiving the same things that I was. However, Muller is very cautious about it, as he is a highly respected experimental physicist, and he does not like to go out into understandings of unproved theory.

Muller, I believe is absolutely correct. Space being stretched out by God also causes time to be stretched out. So it is clear to me that the stretching of time drives our "feel" of existence through time flowing through the thing Muller called NOW.

Pause in your thinking now and consider the dimensions of time.

Backward Time

Nuclear particles can travel in backward time. Many physicists get muddled by this and ignore the idea, as how can this be, time going backward, or going backward in time. It is still a quandary and different theories try to explain what nuclear particles are doing, such as imagining negative energy fields and other seemingly preposterous ideas.

Yes, particles travel backward in time. An electron traveling backward in time is called a positron. It seems all kinds of particles can travel in backward time. These particles are usually called anti-matter.

When a particle and an anti-particle collide there is an explosion into energy with the production of photons. Photons travel at the speed of light where there is no time. That is, photons go about in zero time, as measured from the earth. Clocks on photons, if we could put them there, never measure any time. They, so to speak, dwell in continuous NOW, rattling around in the universe and not needing any time to do their thing.

Biblical Accounts of Time Dilation

The Bible gives two accounts, when time went backward and when time stood still. The Prophet Isaiah records an event where, King Hezekiah of the Jewish Kingdom developed a nasty boil and asked for help from the prophet. (Isaiah 38) The Prophet received a message from God, and came and told the King to put his house in order and prepare to die. The King put his face to the wall in his bedroom and cried to the Lord God and groaned and moaned and told the Lord about all the good things he had done. The Lord listened and told the prophet to go back to the King and tell him, OK, you can have fifteen more years.

The King asked how can I know this for sure; give me a sign? The prophet told him the sun's shadow on the steps of Ahaz will go back ten steps. Think about this for a minute. Most believing people will either say it is a miracle or otherwise say it is an illusion. Unbelievers will just say this proves the Bible to be nonsense. But this event has been recorded for us as something that actuality happened. There is visible evidence. It was recorded for posterity. So what happened?

I suggest the NOW of time went into backward mode so the sun reversed its trajectory direction as seen from the earth, and the shadow produced by the sun cast on the King's steps went back the other way. If you consider other possibilities as the earth reversing its rotation or other such phenomena, that generates all kinds of physical events very difficult to think about.

The second account is when the armies of the children of Israel lead by Joshua need more time to defeat their enemies when they were conquering the land of Cannon, so Joshua commanded the sun to stand still. (Joshua 10:12-15) God listened. Both the sun and the moon stood still for about a whole additional day while the army of Joshua completed their task. As usual, the scriptures are very terse and give very little information about this event other than it happened. What really went on there? It is hard to know. Nevertheless the event was recorded in the scriptures of the Hebrews.

In both these events, since God controls the expansion of the universe, or that God instigated or recognized perhaps some local galaxy event of space-time contraction, NOW on the earth stopped proceeding into forward time. This maybe happened perhaps within some local region of the Milky Way galaxy, or perhaps some huge gravity space-time wave from somewhere else came through the galaxy. Nevertheless, from some cause and reflecting on the theories presented herein, space-time in the region of the earth contracted so that NOW seemed to move into backward time in the first example, and where space-time stopped expanding and stood still in the second example.

So here are two events recorded in Hebrew history where time, instead of NOW advancing in some continuous seemingly invariant manner into forward time, continuing as ever did before going to future time, instead NOW stops or proceeds or contracts into backward time.

All is acting like a positron, in that a positron when moving through some experimental physicist's bubble chamber acts like, and is, an electron going in backward time. At least that is the best explanation physicists give of what a positron is --- antimatter positron is an electron traveling backward in time.

Physicists and engineers make many calculations using this backward time principle of quantum physics most every day when making many of the lovely devices we enjoy. They assume backward time travel of particles so as to accurately make calculations of what is predicted to happen in their devices.

Wow! Think about this for a moment. Particle behavior at the microscopic level is such that they can travel backward in time. If particles can do it, then any collection of particles can travel in backward time. So what does this all mean?

NOW is the Fundamental Thing

Let me suggest that NOW is the fundamental thing. NOW can flow forward into time or backward into time. NOW continues and can slow down or speed up depending on space-time expanding or contracting.

NOW is, therefore, the fundamental thing. Whether NOW passes into forward time or into backward time depends on the expansion direction of the universe. As space stretches out, time stretches out, and NOW moves through or expands into forward space-time. If space-time contracts, NOW moves through or contracts into backward space-time.

Space-Time Expanding/Contracting

Do not be surprised by this concept of NOW and space-time expanding or contracting or discard the idea out of hand. Physics has proven this expanding and contracting of space-time is already continuously happening all over the universe. As one mass body moves toward or away from any other mass body, the space-time between them expands or contracts depending on whether the mass body is approaching the other or receding.

In the presence of a mass body space-time contracts as one approaches that body as, for example, a mass body nearing the earth. As one approaches the earth, space-time contracts do to the presence of the earth, so space becomes smaller and time runs slower in what happens to be the NOW in the local frame as one approaches another mass body.

So do not think it is strange or unacceptable that NOW can either move into forward time or into backward time or just stand still. NOW for any mass body is influenced or modified by any other mass body, and also by the velocity of the mass body as it approaches another mass body.

NOW, according to Muller, is the same all over the universe in the location of local time --- local time being understood to be each place of observation and measurement. Consequently, NOW is the most fundamental thing.

We humans dwell on the earth so the history of our NOW to us is the history of the earth. Many, many, wonderful things have happened to the earth to make it such an exquisite place for man to dwell.

The NOW on the earth, from the very small perspective of man, seems to continue on and on as seemingly forever passing into forward time. Only observations from such as Hezekiah's boil problem or a battle where Joshua needed more time to eliminate the enemies of

Israel, seem to interrupt this experience of us earthlings in this flow of time into forward time on the earth.

Physicists, in the course of discovering the essence of the wonderful creation in which we dwell, observe backward time and forward time in real experiments of actual observations. So this effect is very real and not imaginary.

On the other hand there are some other places which seem to have quite a different characteristic of NOW. As an example, consider what is called a black hole. A huge black hole seems to be present in the mass center of our galaxy, The Milky Way, in which the earth is located within the universe.

A black hole cannot be observed because the gravitational force due to the large mass of a black hole is so strong; electromagnetic waves of such as light cannot escape from the black hole. From an observation point on the earth, space-time at the surface of the black hole stops. Time and space at the surface of the black hole are so contracted that they completely stop. There is no space and there is no time on the black hole surface when as it is observed from the earth.

If we could watch and observe a space ship, for example, as it approaches the black hole, we would need an infinite amount of time on the earth to watch the ship touch the surface of the black hole. Thus we will never observe an object like a spaceship going into a black hole

We can only surmise as to what is happening to the ship in its own NOW frame as it approaches the black hole. We surmise it is shredded into oblivion and turned into nothing we can understand.

On the other hand think about no time and no space, and perhaps huge heat and huge pressure in the black hole. That sounds like hell with no possibility of movement and no passing of time. God has perhaps here given us a picture of hell.

Universal NOW & Flat Space-Time

So what has happened and what is happening in our NOW on the surface of the earth where we humans dwell? God has provided us with a spectacular place to observe and learn about the universe. Space-time here on the earth is almost flat, a consequence of the solar system being near the edge of the Milky Way, our distance from the sun, and the mass of the earth.

We can from the earth make observations of almost the whole visible universe and not be subject to extreme space-time dilation or perhaps a better term, space-time curvature. We seem to have been provided with a most perfect place in which to observe the universe.

Think about that for a moment. The book of Romans in the Bible says God has left enough evidence in creation so that man is without excuse. So yes, God has placed the earth in such a place that man can observe the universe. Mankind ignores the vast evidence in observable universe creation at great eternal risk to themselves.

The curvature of space outside our galaxy seems to be extremely flat. So flat, in fact, that some physicists have estimated the size of the universe to be extremely large. The age of the universe is estimated in earth terms from analysis of the light from objects we observe out to as far as we can detect light. This is about 10 to the tenth power in years. (Probably about 1.4 to the 10th power or 14 billion years.)

Beyond this we understand is more of the universe that cannot be observed until more local time has passed. This whole universe size is estimated by some physicists to be 10 to the 112th power in years. This is a stupendous size. Now we understand the universe is still expanding, and in fact the expansion is accelerating. The fantastic extravagance of God manifesting his extreme power and glory is astounding.

History - Time Dimension NOW

Consider the history of NOW. What has happened in and through NOW cannot be changed. Some of man sometimes think of the possibility of going backward in history and perhaps change the past. Lots of fun fiction in stories and movies has imagined what happens when people attempt to develop time machines and other such imaginations so as to go backward into a period in history. History, however, cannot be changed. What has happened in the past of NOW cannot be changed. Understand that stuff going forward in time or backward in time has nothing to do with history of what has happened.

NOW is independent of which way local time flows. Understand that. NOW is a time dimension as well as forward time and backward time. Thus there are three time dimensions. Space and time are one and the same thing and are called space-time. You cannot have one without the other. You must not think of possibilities in one without the equivalent possibilities in the other. That is what the Michaelson/Morley experiment ultimately proved. NOW and space are merged into one space-time.

According to postulated string theory each space dimension is tied up with two additional highly curved space dimensions. Similarly, NOW is also tied up with what seems to be highly curved backward and forward time.

SEVENTEEN

Entanglement

Theories of quantum physics in some detail were developed during the 1920s. Erwin Schroeder developed the very important quantum physics equations, described by another researcher of quantum physics, Leonard Schiff, which also described fundamental particles as wave functions[19].

Concept of Entanglement

The principle of entanglement in quantum physics conveys the idea of wave functions being superimposed so as to become mixed up with each other or become entangled and so influence each other and somehow become connected with each other. So that if one wave function that has become entangled and comes to be changed, then the entangled others also are changed even if elsewhere in the universe. One function changes the other anywhere in the universe even when separated by vast distances. This is called action at a distance.

About the time this revised edition book is being written large sums of money are being spent trying to invent very fast quantum computing which is based on the principle of action at a distance.

Quantum Physics and Spirit

The Physicist, Muller, has suggested that the quantum physics concept of entanglement has a spiritual factor. This is indeed, very, very interesting --- that a great physicist would even suggest this. Probably he suggested this because quantum entanglement is impossible to understand in logical terms using the past physics thinking about the universe.

The psychological academic world has stumbled over trying to understand the spiritual essence of man even though man's spirituality has been obvious for centuries. This is astounding because the Hebrew Scriptures have given a fuzzy, yet understandably clear picture of what man is. Man is composed of body, soul, and spirit. And deep within the spirit is the heart.

As was discussed previously, a fuzzy representation of man is portrayed by the Tabernacle of the Jews. (Exodus Chapters 25-27) Moses was commanded by God to build the Tabernacle when out in the wilderness as the Hebrews left Egypt to head for the Promised Land. As discussed in other places in this book the Tabernacle portrays the physical body as the home for the soul, and also the gateway to the soul. The soul is the gateway to the spirit, and deep within the spirit is the heart.

Few psychologists and psychiatrists understand this. This Hebrew insight provided by God has been largely ignored.

But now comes this well-known physics experimentalist, Muller, and suggests the spirit world is somehow entangled with the real physical world. He concludes this through his understanding of quantum physics. What an interesting valuable insight. So how does this work, and is there any way this can be experimentally established? Probably not as spiritual things normally cannot be written down in logical terms. Nevertheless, this is a very valuable insight.

So review and consider again the spirt world so as to understand what Muller is trying to say, and then conclude as to the truth of Muller's suggestion as to empathy being the connecting element of the real world to the spirit world.

The Tabernacle understanding of man as composed of body, soul, spirit, and heart comes about by considering the furniture God commanded Moses to put into the Tabernacle. The courtyard area contained an altar for sacrifice and a large basin for washing. These functions occur in that fourfold world-realm of the body of flesh, that of real physical existence.

Then from the courtyard there was a curtain to a tent building which had two rooms --- the rooms separated by another very elaborate curtain. In the first room were a lamp-stand for light, and a table upon which were bread, and an altar for burning special incense oil. These are representations of the functions of the soul --- the altar of incense representing prayers of the mind, the lamp-stand for light for understanding of the mind, and the shew bread for feeding the understanding of the mind. The soul is defined as the mind, will, and emotions. Jesus Christ said I am the bread of life. Jesus Christ said I am the light of the world.

Behind the second very elaborate curtain was a room within which was a box, which had a lid, and attached to the lid and upon it were statue representations of spirits, called angels, cherubim, which indicated the spirit nature of the world-realm of this room. Two angels were bending over slightly, looking at the box surface with their wings extended, with a small gap between the wings of one cherub from the other.

The elaborate curtain between the rooms suggests the soul room is separated from the spirit room and the respective rooms have distinctive separate functions. Yet the soul is the gateway to the spirit as symbolized by and through this curtain.

The box in the spirit room contained the Law (The Ten Commandments) written on stone given to Moses by God, a golden jar of some manna, a food the Israelites collected from the ground in the wilderness, and a stick of almond wood which budded and produced almonds overnight, representing being chosen. Aaron, Moses brother was the proven chosen High Priest through the overnight budding of this rod.

So in this box are symbols of what is the function of the heart of man, the underlying motives of man, and the rules for living successfully, with love and empathy and respect for others of mankind as mandated by the law.

Yes, here is represented, spirit motivation for love of God, respect of God, and of a high quality life for the heart of the God loving person. Here is God given motivation through spiritual food for the heart's understanding of life, and the symbol that the heart person has been chosen by God for eternal life.

The whole tabernacle thing conveyed to the Israelites the idea and understanding that God was present with them. There was the Shekinah Glory present in the gap between the wings of the cherubim. God spoke directly to Moses from this gap. There was the pillar of cloud by day and the pillar of fire at night hovering over the Tabernacle.

The tabernacle thing gave a fuzzy picture of the structure of what is man --- and in particular, the pre-incarnated man, Jesus Christ, pictured as a representation of God.

This is an extremely brief statement and description of the tabernacle. For details and understanding of this portrayal, refer to the previous chapters of this book.

One of the great insights that one can derive from study and consideration of the tabernacle is that the physical realm is quite separated from the spirit realm. Any communication between the physical fourfold world-realm and the spirit fourfold world-realm must go through the soul fourfold world-realm. This understanding is very important. Spiritual beings cannot act directly in the physical realm. Spiritual input from spiritual beings must go through the soul and otherwise influence only the soul so as to cause the soul to direct the body to act and do what the spiritual being desires.

This design by God provides a tremendous protection for man from evil spiritual beings. Evil spiritual beings cannot touch or cause evil things to happen to man except through some human soul, that the spiritual beings, known as demons, have managed to get control of. This provides a wonderful protection for man.

Jesus, while on the earth, spent time casting demons out of people. This seems very strange to us moderns. Most of us seem to have no contact with demons so we think they do not exist. Demons are apparently evil spirits and cohorts of that great enemy of God, Satan.

Demons do not seem to infect animals. Jesus cast out a legion of demons from a deranged man living among some tombs. When Jesus was about to do it, the demons knowing who He is, used the voice of the man to plead with Jesus not to send them to the Pit, but that they be allowed to go into a very large nearby herd of swine. Jesus did what they wanted, cast them out of the man and into the swine, and immediately, the swine (The record says about 2000 of them.) ran down a steep cliff into a lake and drowned.

One wonders why this story is in the Bible. Jesus wants to teach us. Thus this story explains a little about the demon spirit realm. Therefore, since we understand devil's and demon's goals are to kill as many people as possible, it seems to give us the idea that demons do not infect or occupy animals --- or to continue to live within animals, as the swine promptly killed themselves.

Jesus' stories usually have several meanings and application for teaching. The healed demon possessed man became quite a preacher telling everybody his story as, subsequently; very many people in this region became followers of Jesus.

Thus understand that the spiritual world-realm is completely separate from the physical world-realm and one realm cannot influence the other except through some human soul.

Muller's Entanglement of Spirit

So given Muller's suggestion that quantum physics entanglement has a spiritual thing about it, which he reduced to empathy, and the tabernacle picture of the heart world-realm within the spirt world-realm with its principles for living, love, and empathy for fellow man, and the loving relationship with God, what are we to make of the quantum physics contribution of entanglement to the spirit world-realm?

Entanglement Revelation and Flat Space-Time

Understand as was established in the previous chapter that NOW is the engine for discovery revelation in the physics of entanglement. As was shown by the Copenhagen understanding of entanglement, discovery revelation is the quandary of the event when the Schrodinger Cat box is opened, and the wave functions of quantum physics collapse into probably distributions. As was established herein, all of the wave functions of everything exist everywhere in the universe. These wave functions are all entangled. So as NOW proceeds into forward time, or backward time, or slows down into continuous NOW, entanglement discovery revelation happens.

As the vast cat box of the universe, like Schrodinger's Cat Box, is opened by discovery revelation through NOW, all the wave functions collapse into probabilities, and the universe proceeds on into stretched out or shrinking space-time, or into the same space-time, with new or revised probability distributions.

NOW the Process of Entanglement Revelation

Thus NOW is the process of entanglement revelation. Time and space of space-time expand or contract, stretch or shrink, thus causing the movement of NOW forward or backward, either fast or slowly, or not at all.

This happens all over the universe almost simultaneously, because the NOW of every place in the universe are essentially the same NOW, according to Muller, in regions of the universe where the space-time curvature is nearly flat. This has been caused, essentially, because the universe is so tremendously expanded and space-time outside of galaxies is so extremely flat,

Because of the spooky nature of this entanglement, Muller called it spiritual. I suggest it is just the nature of the operation of the universe. It is just the physical reality of the universe fourfold world-realm. Everything in the universe in its own local time essentially has the same NOW compared to any other place in the universe in regions of nearly flat space-time. That is a very important insight to understanding the relation of entanglement to NOW. Yes, as NOW unfolds the wave functions are revealed all over the universe, and they all have nearly the same NOW.

It is only when an observer tries to observe some other place in the universe from his own NOW that the principles of relativity, space expansion/contraction, and time dilation happen, so any observer observes the rest of the universe within the observed object's retarded time and contracted space, really just retarded space-time.

Wow! God is magnificent! What a marvelous universe He has created through the mind of Jesus Christ.

Empathy a Factor of Quantum Physics?

So let us now go back to Muller's suggestion of empathy as a factor of quantum physics in the generation of spookiness of reality entanglement. Muller suggested that the ability to imagine yourself as someone else, the ability to sort of put yourself in someone's else' shoes, and so to imagine you are them, and, therefore, have concern for them and their welfare, is the essence of the empathy implied from the spookiness of quantum physics, the Copenhagen interpretation. This Muller theorized because of action at a distance, (simultaneous action perhaps million billion billion of miles apart) which in the minds of a lot of physicists, violates relativity theory, and is, therefore, considered spooky.

Jesus gave us a very similar concept to Muller's empathy. Jesus said, "You shall love your neighbor as yourself." (Mark12:31) This statement is a main tenant of Christian Gospel. The whole Christian Gospel consists of all that the Bible teaches, and that we are to love God and love one another, and Jesus gave a further command, "Love one another even as I have loved you". (John 13:34)

So we are to love people as Jesus loved people. That is probably impossible, yet Jesus gave us this command. As we Christians pursue our lives, we are to treat people as Jesus treated people. We are to manifest the virtues of a righteous spirit --- love, joy, peace, patience, kindness, goodness, faithfulness, gentleness, self-control. (Galatians 5:22)

So the Christian Gospel contains the essence of the supposed spookiness of quantum physics. What an astounding revelation. Indeed, man is without excuse. Man must, therefore, recognize God through a little understanding of quantum physics.

This whole Christian concept is vastly more than just empathy. Manifested out into the world, this empathy, derived from the Gospel, is the essence of the very successful Christian culture. People in the West have lived within Christian culture so long they do not even understand or even conceive of the ramifications of non-Christian cultures.

The concept of the heart as described by the contents of the box in the Tabernacle, the Law (spiritual principles for living with much included empathy), spiritual food from God, spiritual assurance of being chosen, are the essential things of spiritual entanglement for mankind.

These are some of what Muller calls unproven truths. Quantum entanglement demonstrates the unproven truths of God operating and maintaining the universe of space-time.

One of the greatly misunderstood conundrums in our modern American culture is the lack of understanding of spirit. Most people think in terms of ghosts and spooky stuff when thinking about the spirit. Most of mankind do not think they even have a spirit. The bible says that when God created man, God inserted spirit into dust (dust being stuff of physical reality) and man became a living soul. (Geneses 2:7) So understand that the source of a lot of confusion in modern understanding is because the psychological intellectual academic world, and even Christians thinkers and academics, have not clearly defined what man is.

The Bible says man is composed of spirit, soul, and body. The spirit clearly has different functions than the functions of the soul, the soul being the thinking mind, will, and emotions. The heart, as suggested by the understanding of the Bible through the tabernacle analogy, is the thing that Muller reduced to empathy. The heart is deep within the spirit, and is, in fact, the entanglement factor in Muller's type of approach to the existence of empathy within the human person.

Not Spirit Action at a Distance

But action at a distance has nothing to do with spirituality. Action at a distance is just the normal operation of the space-time universe. This is the way God made the universe. Some young clever experimental physicist will soon prove this, and in the process perhaps earn a Nobel Prize.

Me as a Wave Function

I am quite intrigued by the concept of Me as a wave function of quantum physics. I sit on the deck of my home and watch the Salmon River go by at flood stage of about 80,000 cubic feet per second, carrying huge logs and mud along for the ride, along with once in a while, some extreme adventurers in rafts and kayaks, running the very cold river for the fun, excitement, and challenge of it.

The surface water waves surge and fluctuate with white caps constantly curving and boiling over in a beautiful, powerful canopy of noise and beauty. Waves are beautiful mesmerizing things to watch. Time seems to stand still.

When as a kid and near being a teenager, I sat for hours and hours on end, on a rock on the Pacific Ocean watching the waves surge back and forth up and down, creating repetitive crashing sounds that filled my ears with quiet contentment. My hand is on a fishing pole waiting and watching, Me being mesmerized by the spellbinding beauty and form.

I must not take my eyes off of the ocean for more than four seconds at a time, as a rogue wave might get me and wash me off the rock to my ugly early prospective demise. It is almost impossible to climb back out of the ocean due to the huge fluctuating water level with each wave and the sharp cutting edges of mussel shells of the mussels living on the rocks. Many a flatlander, (Those from the Bay Area of California, or elsewhere), drowned while fishing from the rocks.

I very much enjoyed the focused alertness and my solitude and daydreaming. My mother would be happy too if I brought home a few fish. It was important to keep my mother happy as then I had the freedom to wander about the earth, observe and do everything that was interesting, and so create my own thing. This is indeed a most astounding thing of the wonderful life of freedom come to pass in the United States of America.

The waves surged back and forth in an endless canopy of sound, form, and color. Waves of sound, water, or anything else for that matter, are similar and have common characteristics.

Later in life I thought of ways electromagnetic waves, in my imagination of them, could be shuffled, bent around, and slowed down so that some tiny component of the wave would synchronize with my powerful electron beam, so that the beam would perform work on a tiny part of the wave. This would quite amplify the whole wave and so provide my employer with a marvelous device useful to the military of the United States, for which they would pay a goodly sum. So my employer paid me a rather handsome wage. Sometimes even, I received a real bonanza, a stock option on the company stock that rose in price in a wonderful heartwarming trend.

Memories come to me that stir up a joyful happiness of being at the beach at Waikiki, enjoying the wonderful repetition of just perfect surf waves to ride again and again to my heart's content. Ah, yes, great memories of most wonderful waves.

So now in my old age of life I have come to understand I am a composite wave of some stuff of quantum physics spreading out all over the universe --- very, very intriguing. What does this all mean?

Yes, I make all kinds of waves. As I move back and forth and dance all around, I make waves in space-time. If I yell in happy exuberance, I make sound waves. I throw a rock at the river. I make water waves. The auto and truck traffic on the highway above my home make all kinds of sound waves, somewhat interrupting otherwise good thoughts, and sometimes are a little disturbing.

So am I really a wave dancing around in space-time, and is my quantum physics wave dancing and fluctuating up and down and sideways like the river or the ocean, or even like some amplified electromagnetic microwave power spreading out over the earth and even out into the universe?

Somewhere in the universe or even outside the universe, is my own quantum physics wave, being examined like I examine and watch the river waves and the ocean waves, and maybe like, as I think about it in the imagination of my mind, a powerful microwave electromagnetic wave?

Am I being watched for my free-will decisions and my free-will acts committed in space-time?

Wow! Yes, yes, indeed! I am being watched! Very, very, interesting!

All this understanding insight should make one very, very, cautious --- especially about one's deep thinking and behavior.

Causality

So now let us go back and again consider the concept that started all this discussion --- that of causality. God is omnipotent and rules --- not one hair shall fall from my head without the will of God. It has been established that you and I have free will. God has given me free will so I will make good and bad decisions. How is it that God outside of space-time interacts within space-time so that my free will decisions are really free will decisions and not some imaginary thing?

From the Tabernacle illustration there is a room like thing where my spirit has a home within my body, and it contains the box of my heart. If I am a Christian, God's Spirit comes and makes a home within me and lives within my spirit and protects me from evil spirits. If I am not a Christian, evil spirts and demons have access to my spirit. Remember, the spirit-realm is not part of space-time creation.

God's Spirit present within Christian's spirit can fill Christian's heart box with His love so Christian's motivations become like God's desired motivations. From the presence of God's Spirit in Christian's spirit (symbolized by the enclosed room) there is communication entanglement into the room of the soul of Christian. The washed clean Christian heart knows God's Spirit presence, and since the Christian heart through Christian's spirit in the presence of God's Spirit, gives or directs thoughts and ideas to Christian's soul, God loves Christian. And, of course, Christian's soul directs Christian's body in physical space-time so body does what soul tells it to do.

So God outside of space-time does not cause anything within space-time. Understand; I am not limiting God in any way. This is just the character of God, just like God is not capable of doing evil. It is contrary to His being.

NOW History

The history of NOW is laid out in the books of God's records that He keeps outside of space-time. A new NOW begins where the history in the recorded books left off. The wave functions are there to be revealed for the advance of space-time into forward time dimension or into backward time dimension, or stand still. Free will decisions are made and NOW happens as the wave functions collapse into probabilities. God controls each particular item of probability distribution selection, and can select anything to happen subject to probability distribution.

God controls by selection the outcome of every roll of dice so God controls and directs the result, and chooses any point in any statistical distribution. God does not directly cause anything within space-time, yet He determines the outcome point in the distribution of possibilities.

Understand my thinking. I am not limiting God in any way whatsoever. God is omnipotent and, therefore, can do anything He pleases. God is unfathomable and past understanding. My intention is not in any way to add to the Scriptures of the Holy Bible. What I am trying to do is to give you some understanding of the awesomeness of God. As the Apostle Paul said in the Book of Romans:

Man is without excuse.

This description of the characteristics of the physical universe is intended to give you a little insight into a little of how God through his Son, the Lord Jesus Christ, made and rules the universe and sustains the universe, so as to make a place for man to dwell and, therefore, come to know God.

EIGHTEEN

Eternity

Consider now the consequences of all this discussion, and the consequences of the established facts, and the truth of the logical thinking thereby enabled.

Jesus Christ: Intersection of Space-Time and Eternity

Understand that Jesus Christ is an intersection of eternity and space-time. We do not understand this with our minds, but somehow Jesus Christ left his eternal home outside of space-time and dwelt among men for a season within space-time. This, of course, is the Christian Gospel.

The Christian Gospel is, to a great extent, based on the revelations God gave to the Hebrews. Fuzzy pictures like the Tabernacle teach us about God through these scripture writings of the Jews. The Christian Gospel based on the Bible teaches that before the end of the present earth, many Jews will accept the blessings of Jesus Christ, and become part of Christ's most Holy Church --- the Universal Gathering of all believers in Jesus Christ.

Jesus while living on the earth demonstrated what it is in the life of man that God approves and loves. Jesus walked about on the earth gathering and teaching multitudes about God. Jesus demonstrated who He is, the Creator of the space-time universe, by healing the sick, fixing broken people, meeting people in their ugly lives, and searching for their basic needs of both mind and spirit. Jesus loved people. Jesus highly respected women as well as men and revealed his resurrected eternal body first to a woman rather than to his disciples.

Jesus healed people at a distance. He did not need to be present at the location of the sufferer to effect restoration of body and soul. Remember that space-time is Jesus' creation and He is very gentle with it, but His understanding of it enabled Him to use it to accomplish great things to provide knowledge to people as to who He is and so bring people to worship Him. God cannot lie; it is against His nature. Thus Jesus accepted worship of Himself by all kinds of people.

Jesus said there are three witnesses for establishing who He is. First the witness He gives of Himself, second the witness of the prophet, John the Baptist, who proclaimed Him to be the Lamb of God, and third the powerful astounding miracles He did in themselves, which showed that he controlled events in space-time, such as healing diseases. He traveled from one place to another instantaneously without needing intervening time, perhaps in a similar way as to a selection of a potential event in the distribution of a wave function, wherein He controlled wind and waves of water. He knew what other people were thinking in their minds.

Yes, Jesus proved while he was on the earth that He is The Creator God of the universe in the flesh of a man.

After His death and resurrection, the disciples He left behind went out into the world at great risk to themselves to tell the world about Jesus. All but John died as martyrs. These disciples knew who Jesus is and gave their earthly lives to His cause. They knew Him to be God in the flesh of a man.

Preparation for Eternity

Wow! What opportunity man has on the earth to learn to hate evil and do good and prepare the self for eternity. A new Christian, a believer in Jesus Christ by faith, is given the gift of righteousness, that is, right standing with God. He or she is forgiven of all sins and trespasses and then stands before God blameless. Yes, so what will Christian do with this initial grubstake, or down payment of righteousness? Yes, Christian, respond. Love God! Love brothers and sisters in Christ. Love your neighbors. Be a faithful witness of what God has done in your Christian life.

Life is full of grief and misery and encounters with evil done through the free will of others of man, but with the presence of God's Spirit within Christian's spirit, all things are possible, and life can become full of peace, fragrance, and beauty.

Peace is for the Christian's soul; Christian is a sweet fragrance to the nostrils of God; Christian has a beautiful spirit presented by Christian to the world, demonstrating what it is to be a Christian.

Embryo Insertion of Spirit

When I was conceived within my mother, God inserted my spirit into an embryo from my mother which was activated by my father, was nurtured and grew, matured, and became me. I became a person with a body in the universe of space-time, in what I have been calling the physical world-realm.

Jesus Christ, the Son of God, now dwells in what the Apostle Paul calls, Heavenly Places or Heavenly Realms. Paul says that the, "Me", inside my mother, was chosen in Him, Jesus Christ, before the foundation of the world, and that I should be holy and blameless.

Yes, indeed! Given the understanding I am trying to give to you, since Jesus Christ's first coming to earth was an event in the intersection of the Eternity of the Heavenly Places with space-time in the world-realm of physical creation, then there happened an event that God instigated, inserting my spirit into the embryo, so the embryo from my mother and father became me, and I am a fourfold man of body, soul, spirit, and heart within the fourfold realms.

If "Me" is a composite wave function in quantum physics space time, as has been established herein, then the wave function of Me, now not only spreads out all across space-time in physical creation, but also like that of my Lord Jesus Christ, spreads across the Heavenly Places.

And in some marvelous way, I have been joined to my Lord Jesus Christ in the spirit. (I Corinthians 6:17)

Spirit is not part of space-time. Yet it seems my spirit in the fourfold spirit-realm, and my soul in the fourfold soul-realm in the fourfold space-time of the fourfold world-realm of physical creation, are entangled.

This is very, very, interesting. My spirit, given to me by God, through Jesus Christ, is then also entangled within what I call Eternity, and Paul called Heavenly Places. Therefore, my eternal life with Jesus Christ has already been going on outside of space-time, and I have been joined to Jesus Christ in the Holy Body of Christ's Universal Church in the Heavenly Places.

So I must conclude that since my spirit which came from God, and was given to me by God, and so already existed in eternity, then I know I am already now in eternity with my new spiritual body outside of space-time.

That is, I am entangled with Jesus Christ. The composite wave function that is me is entangled with the stupendous composite wave function of Jesus Christ, so that when my body of flesh, living in the world-realm of the flesh dies, so like the Cat in Schroeder's Box, as the box is opened by observation of my death, my wave function in quantum physics space-time collapses into the eternity of Me in my spiritual body in eternity. Yes, astounding! Praise Jesus!

Now I am not providing you with any very esoteric mathematical expressions with hard to understand mathematical equations to prove all this like a good physicist would. That is not the intention of this writing.

Nevertheless, consider what is evident in the creation of space-time, that God has said that enough evidence has been provided by creation in space-time, so that man is without excuse --- man must, therefore, search for God.

The Bible says that God will give the presence of the Holy Spirit to those who will ask for it. Thus it is imperative that you, dear reader, search for God. Come by faith in Jesus Christ, confess your sins and trespasses, confess that you are indeed guilty of all such wickedness and accept by faith the love of Jesus Christ for the complete forgiveness of all your sins, shortcomings, and trespasses.

The Christian life is not necessarily easy. God just loves to discipline and work on Christian so that he or she is polished into a fantastic person of peace, fragrance, and beauty. Now that is something both you and God want and desire.

This Christian life will be a fantastic trip. Many years ago, when I was under the teaching of Pastor Ray Stedman at the Peninsula Bible Church, in Palo Alto, California, he was preaching on the Bible book of Ecclesiastes. He preached:

"Put all you have into life and accomplish anything you desire."

At least that is how I interpreted it! So I launched my life into what the world would think was a big effort to obtain huge success.

As I look back on it, life was a fantastic trip, full of success, full of trials and tribulations, and encounters with evil. All through it all, Jesus Christ, with the presence of the Holy Spirit within me, lead me, seemingly intervened when I was about to do something really stupid, protected me, and watched over me through all my successes, failures, trials, and tribulations.

In my case it was not easy. Using my free will I made some very bad mistakes. Nevertheless, I eventually grew into a person possessed of peace --- peace in my soul. Therefore, I know I belong to the vast eternal Universal Church of Jesus Christ, and am joined to Jesus Christ. I deeply love Him with all my heart, my spirit, my soul, and the strength of my body.

I recall a movie I watched years ago. In it some Mexican vaqueros were watching some gringo adventurers debark on a very perilous journey. They shouted out in Spanish, "Vaya con Dios" --- may God be with you. They perhaps intended it as sarcasm. It could have been interpreted as such, or be interpreted as providing a blessing for the journey.

So also it is with you. Reject Jesus Christ at great peril. Indeed, may God be with you as you embark and conduct the adventure of life.

NINETEEN

Vision Quest

On the cover of this book is a picture of the Seven Devils Mountains of Idaho. The highest in the group are a pair, She Devil on the right and He Devil on the left of the pass between them. Native Americans in past times sought their spirit vision of life through questing about in these mountains.

Your Christian spirit vision for life comes to you by asking for it from the Holy Spirit of God. The Holy Spirit sent by your Lord Jesus Christ and God the Father, has come to you to have a home within your spirit, live within you, comfort you, and bless you. Yes, a very wonderful, marvelous, experience of wholesome spiritual life in fellowship with the only God, Mighty and Supreme, comes to you. This All Mighty God continually awaits you, the Christian.

Your spirit deep within you, however, needs to have its own vision, meaning a spiritual path to follow for the rest of your life.

But you have this astounding free will that is directed by your soul. The inputs from your body of flesh, mind and emotions, encounters with evil, and from the evil exercise of the free will of others of mankind, all can much confuse and corrupt your spirit vision. So now consider some possibilities and discombobulations.

Put on your imagining hat and imagine you are in your spiritship of life seemingly flying along approaching the wicked devils of life. He Devil and She Devil in front of you and myriads of other little spirit devils are scattered around in the rocks and cliffs of life. You are making your God given freewill choices of your life. Are you going to make it through all the devils, in between the gaps in the approaching devil mountains, in your spiritship and proceed onto your place before the throne of God in the distant heavenly blue, or are you going to crash on the rocks?

Yes? No? Maybe?

Consider some examples of real history. Consider the life of Gideon in the Bible book of Judges. Very bad things are happening to the Israelite nation. God recruits Gideon in a spectacular way and he has astounding success defeating the enemies of God who were persecuting, robing, and suppressing the Israelite tribes. To understand the situation completely you best read the account in Judges, Chapters 6, 7, and 8. After tremendous success in the Kingdom of God defeating the enemies, Gideon moves on and finishes out the last 40 years of his life on earth.

The Israelites want to make him king. He says no, and in a pious way tells them, "No, let God rule over you." But then Gideon acts like a king, taxes them to acquire gold, acquires a harem, rules with cruelty, and does a power trip murdering some fearful people who did not show him proper respect. Yes, he has an astounding wreck of spirit on the He Devils and She Devils of life so generating great evil in lives of fellow Israelites, and worst of all, corrupts the fellowship and worship of his fellow Israelites.

Gideon finishes life badly.

As another example, my own blood brother (I was the youngest of four boys with a younger sister) who was an extremely good mentor, caregiver, and counselor to me while I was growing up, achieved astounding success laboring in the Kingdom of God in the mosquito infested swamps of Papua New Guinea. He translated the Bible into a native language, built schools, created huge amounts of curriculum for the schools in the trade language used in Papua New Guinea, established medical care, created econometric mechanisms for prosperous indigenous native life, created native run business enterprises for building, construction, transportation logistics, and doing many other things --- yes, a very fruitful Christian life, simply astounding, benefiting thousands of people.

Then like Gideon, after 40 years or so he moves on. He becomes judgmental, becomes cruel, intolerant of input from others, falls victim to making money fast schemes run by crooks, which, of course, lead to disaster, yet in his mind he was still doing everything for the Kingdom of God. He spiritually wrecked and scattered his convolutions about. All is similar to that end of life pursued by Gideon even Gideon's lust for gold.

Yes, like Gideon, he finishes life badly.

Will that happen to you?

Consider also some pastors of mega churches in our present times. Years of huge ministry success bringing in large numbers of people into the Kingdom of God by their preaching and leadership. Then like Gideon some attempt to acquire a harem, which in our day must be done very discretely. But in arrogance and pride they get careless and it gets discovered to their disaster and the disaster of the Churches they served.

Yes, more crashes onto the He Devils and She Devils of life.

I found a friend in my land selling days when I would leave the land office for an hour or so on Sunday to attend a very small nearby church. The friend was an interesting complex person, full of a lot of ideas, a dumpster diver where he salvaged lots of stuff to build his yard, house, and outbuildings. His maximum speed when driving on a main highway was 45 miles per hour while the speed limit was 65, so becoming a road hazard. He barely watered his yard plants or fertilized them. They had to survive on their own. He was always cutting costs, controlling his wife and just in general did his own thing. He did not want his wife to have a computer or to have her get a job, while he even scraped and saved every penny that came along. He once went to the church deacons and complained his wife did not obey him properly.

But he could discuss and argue on most any subject with great alacrity. He obtained the Wall Street Journal out of the dumpster most every day so he was well informed and a very interesting conversationalist. I very much enjoyed him as a friend, and yes, putting up with his eccentricities.

He had left Michigan and came to Idaho where he wanted to hunt and fish. His wife became a Christian in Idaho, and not long after that so did he.

As the years went by he became more mature as a Christian and grew in his walk with the Lord and became involved in church leadership and its conflict's. We became good friends and he grew in the faith and the love of the Lord Jesus.

Twenty years after our friendship started, and about 40 years after becoming a Christian, while my wife and I were wintering in California, we learned my friend had died. On our return home his wife told me he got a severe case of kidney stones with very severe pain. Lots of frustration with the Veterans Administration got him inadequate medical care. After several trips to the local emergency room with the answer some more pain killing pills, he gave up and shot himself.

He wrecked.

Now I know a little about kidney stones as my wife went through four months of intense medical system struggle with four hospital applied ultrasound blasts and two laser blasts to explode and pulverize the stones and still not getting rid of all of them. I always ask lots of questions so one of the doctors involved gave me an outstanding educational blow by blow account of what was happening with x-ray pictures and sonograms. Kidney stones hurt a lot with very severe pain as the sharp spires on them irritate the walls of the urine tube while moving to the bladder. But they eventually usually pass and hers finally did.

I was very sad to have lost my friend, and I even became angry at his memory as I no longer had him around for the deep discussions, including spiritual ones, that I had very much enjoyed. How is it that a Christian with about 40 years of progressing Christian life, decides to become God, or maybe angry at God, or angry at the world, usurps God's power, and so by exercising his free will, murders himself?

Yes, another wreck on the devil rocks of life.

There are many other examples of men and women who have lived exemplary Christian lives and near the end of life wrecked.

"Some Christian men become quite foolish in their old age", reported my father to me, from observations he had made during his lifetime. Father had a very faithful ministry of the Gospel in a large denomination over many years in several churches. Yes, those Christian men all seemingly still believed the Christian faith, believed themselves were doing well in the Kingdom of God, but somehow are deceived by He Devils and She Devils, and wreck.

Then consider the life of King David, a man after God's own heart as reported by the Bible. David wrote many, many very precious psalms that are in the Bible and are so comforting to vast numbers of Christian people. His ministry was extremely successful, his kingship extremely successful.

He seemingly retires from the stress of military campaigns and is strolling on his palace roof and sees a beautiful woman bathing. Lust gets the best of him even though he has half dozen or so wives, so he gets her fetched. It's a long story and you best read the full account in the Bible.

Yes, a wreck.

David commits adultery and then commits murder to cover it all up. But David's conscience speaks to him and he is quite disquieted. The Lord sends a prophet to confront him with a little parallel story.

David pronounces judgement on the culprit in the story and the prophet tells him, you, King David, no less, are the guilty, sinful man. David confesses and repents.

David is forgiven, but the prophet tells him what will be the consequences of his crimes. The crimes will bring corruption and destruction to his sons, to his family, to the community of the Israelites, and his kingdom. During all this which then, subsequently, happened, David would come to very severe, almost over whelming grief.

Similarly, wrecks can happen in our own lives. Through confession and repentance our sins are forgiven and life goes on. But sins have very nasty consequences that bring on lots of pain and destruction to family, friends, neighbors, and even the country.

What is the solution?

The solution is to cultivate and cling to a Christ centered vision for life on earth. Let your vision quest be driven by understanding the Holy Scriptures given to you by the Holy Spirit of God. Let your mind be enveloped by the fruits of the spirit --- love, joy, peace, patience, kindness, goodness, faithfulness, fullness, gentleness, self-control, all imperatives given to us in the Bible. With your mind in control of your actions, direct your body and speech to practice these fruits of the spirit.

Remember the path of life of the true Christian --- first heart washing and cleansing, then the Spirit of God coming to live within your spirit, then your soul acquiring moral excellence, knowledge, and self-control, then your body obeying your mind conducting perseverance, godliness, and kindness. Again, these imperatives are given by the Apostle Peter in 2 Peter: 1: 5-7.

Let your mind and spirit exercise the spiritual gifts you have been given by the Holy Spirit. If you are not sure of the spiritual gifts you have been given, talk to a few sincere Lord Jesus loving Christian friends. The gift is probably something you have been doing naturally in the course of life and have not fully realized it was a special gift given to you by the Holy Spirit.

Let your spirit vision be committed to using the opportunities that may appear to occur in the course of your life so as to be flexible, adapt to new circumstances with understanding that God is directing these circumstances to you for your benefit, and the benefit of others, and for the benefit of the Kingdom Jesus Christ.

Understand that God lets the spiritually wounded come wandering into your life so you may use your gifts for healing. Some have crashed on the rocky devils of life and lay confused and helpless and in a quandary of what to do. Your gifts received from God the Holy Spirit, are there to be exercised to heal and restore.

Such vision quest, really the deep seated still small voice within you that can give direction and motivation to your life, gives you your own healing and confidence to your own life --- like that of the long-suffering Job of the Bible, so that your life can be filled with peace, fragrance and beauty.

Peace is a state of your mind. When you have peace in your life you know and have confidence that God is working in your life. You then also are a sweet fragrance to God, through knowing that God deeply loves you, you deeply love God. The spiritual beauty of your life is a testimony to those God sends into your life that the work of God is real in you, and from deep down within you, your spiritual beauty gives understanding that God is at work, comforting, healing, and building lives for the eternal Kingdom of God!

Yes, spend your life cultivating your vision quest. Love God. Love your neighbor as yourself, exercise your spiritual gifts. Do acts of love and kindness for those in the Kingdom of God, your Church, and your neighbors. Overcome evil with good. Forgive those who do you wrong, or do evil to you, or disrespect you. Avoid addictions, keep the faith, exercise faith and trust, and trust God in everything.

Let your vision be all that above, and may it be savored with a meek and quiet spirit.

May the Lord Jesus Christ richly bless you.

Citations

1   Nee, Watchman. *What Shall This Man Do?*   Victory Press, London, Great Britain, 1961

2   Stedman, Ray C. *Expository Studies in 1 John.* Word Books, 1980

3   Whiston, William, A. M., translator. *The Works of Josephus.* Hendrickson Publishers, 1987

4   Hodge, Frederick W. and Lewis, Theodore H. *Spanish Explorers in the Southern United States 1528-1543.* Texas State Historical Association, 1990

5   Prescott, William Hickling. *History of the Conquest of Mexico and the History of the Conquest of Peru.* Random House, 1843, 1847, Modern Library Printing

6   Hudson, Charles. *Knights of Spain, Warriors of the Sun.* The University of Georgia Press, Athens and London, 1997

7   Foster, William C. *Spanish Expeditions into Texas.* University of Texas Press, 1995

8   Nokes, J. Richard. *Columbia's River, The Voyages of Robert Gray, 1787 – 1793.* Washington State Historical Society, 1991

9   Bawlf, Samuel. *The Secret Voyage of Sir Francis Drake, 1577-1580.* Walker and Company, 2003

10 "Executive Documents of the United States House of Representatives." September 1860, Published in the Records of Congress, 1866-1867

11 Robinson, W. W. *Land in California.* University of California Press, 1948

12 Gaca, Kathy L. *The Making of Fornication.* University of California Press, Berkeley, Los Angeles, London, 2003

13 Mackay LL.D., Charles Mackay. *Memoirs of Extraordinary Popular Delusions and the Madness of Crowds.* Richard Bentley, 1841, reprint Farrar, Straus and Giroux, New York, 1932

14 Desiderous Erasmus of Rotterdam. *The Praise of Folly.* Walter J. Black, Inc., 1942

15 Dirac, P. A. M., *The Principles of Quantum Mechanics*, Oxford at the Clarendon Press, 4th Edition 1958

16 Schrodinger's Cat is well explained by Google

17 Stuart J. Freedman and John F. Clauser, Phys. Rev. Lett. **28**, 938 – 3 April 1972

18 Muller, Richard A., *The Physics of Time,* W. W. Norton & Company, 2016

19 Schiff, Leonard I., *Quantum Mechanics*, McGraw-Hill Book Company, Inc, 1955

www.ingramcontent.com/pod-product-compliance
Lightning Source LLC
Chambersburg PA
CBHW061245120726
48001CB00001B/143